SO-EIE-723

diary of a 6th grade ninja

2 BOOKS IN 1!

Includes:

Diary of a 6th Grade Ninja #1

Diary of a 6th Grade Ninja #2: Pirate Invasion

BY MARCUS EMERSON

AND NOAH CHILD, WITH SAL HUNTER

ILLUSTRATED BY DAVID LEE

Literati

Literati ✦ Austin, Texas

Story © 2012 by Emerson House Publishing
Illustrations © 2013 by David Lee
Cover and internal design © 2022 by Literati, Inc.
All rights reserved.

Published by Literati, Inc.
1145 West 5th Austin, TX 78703
Find us online at literati.com & @literati

Paperback ISBN: 978-1-7374508-9-4

Originally published as *Diary of a 6th Grade Ninja* and *Diary of a 6th Grade Ninja #2: Pirate Invasion* by Emerson Publishing House in 2013.

Printed in Canada

This is a work of fiction. Any similarity to actual persons living or dead, business establishments, events, or places is entirely coincidental.

First Edition 10 9 8 7 6 5 4 3 2 1

For my kids . . .

Oh, the life of being a ninja. I know what you're thinking—it's an awesome life filled with secrets, crazy ninja moves, and running on the tops of trees. Well, you're right. I'm not gonna lie to you—it's an absolutely *fantastic* life.

But it wasn't always that way.

This might surprise you, but ninjas are often seen as the *bad* guys. I know, right? I had no idea either until I became one. Though looking back, I should've seen the signs early on. You know what they say—hindsight is 20/20.

So this is my story—my diary . . . er, my *chronicle*. I feel as though it has to be told for others to read so they can learn about the events at Buchanan School. History has to be studied and learned from or else it's destined to repeat itself. And that's something I cannot allow.

My name is Chase Cooper, and I'm eleven years old.

I'm the kind of kid that likes to read comic books and watch old horror movies with my dad. If you were to see me walking down the street, you'd try your best not to bump into me, but only because I'm sorta scrawny. I see all these articles online with titles about losing weight and getting rid of unwanted body fat, and my jaw just drops because I can't gain weight to save my life! I've started working out with my dad when he gets home from work, but it's hard to keep up with him.

All this to say that if you saw me, the last thing you'd think was "dangerous ninja."

I'm not the most popular kid in school, that's for sure. I've never had a girlfriend, and I've never played sports outside of gym class. That's not true—I was on a soccer team in third grade, but after a shin guard to the face and a broken nose, I quit.

So I'm scrawny and unpopular. What else can I apply to those two traits for a completely wretched experience? The *start* of school. But wait! Let's multiply that by a million—I'm also the *new* kid at this particular school.

My parents decided to move across town over the summer so we could live in a slightly larger house. I mean, really? How selfish is *that*? A bigger house, but social death for me! Being in a new district means an entire herd of new students that I don't know.

Well, that's not entirely true either. I know Zoe. She's the same age as me, but doesn't really count because she's my cousin.

Luckily, we had the same gym class together. She was surprised to see me on that first day. I remember it well—it was a Monday, the day I caught my first glimpse of the ninjas at Buchanan.

"Chase?" Zoe asked. She was wearing gym shorts and a tank top with the school's mascot on it.

"Hey, Zoe," I said.

She looked surprised. "It *is* you! What're you doing *here*?"

Going to school, dummy. That's what I *wanted* to say but decided against it. "My parents moved to this side of town, so I go to school here now."

Zoe laughed. "That's so cool! My own cousin in the same school as me! What fun we'll have!"

I looked at her silky hair and perfect skin. She kind of looked like one of those models on teenybopper magazines. Yeah, there was no way she'd keep herself affiliated with the likes of me, but I gave her the benefit of the doubt. "Uh-huh, it'll be great," I sighed.

The coach, Mr. Cooper, was at the front of the gymnasium checking off students he knew. He walked up to the rest and asked for their names and grades. Finally, he approached Zoe and me.

"Good morning, Zoe," Mr. Cooper said as he scraped a check-mark into the attendance list. Then he looked at me. "And what's your name?"

Zoe answered for me. "This is Chase Cooper. He's my cousin," she said with a smile.

"Good to have you here," said Mr. Cooper. Then he pointed at Zoe. "She's a good kid to have as a cousin. It's the start of school, but I've already seen her on several try-out lists. You'll do good to follow her lead."

I faked a smile. "Sure."

As Mr. Cooper walked away, Zoe continued speaking. "Why didn't you tell me you were starting at this school?"

I shrugged my shoulders. "We don't really talk that much, and it never came up in conversation. We hardly ever see each other."

Zoe crinkled her nose. "We see each other *every weekend*. Our families have Sunday brunch together at the park!"

I couldn't argue with her. "It's just a little embarrassing."

"You have nothing to be embarrassed about. Starting a new school might be weird, but it's not like you have the ability to control a situation like that," she said.

I didn't want to tell her I was embarrassed and scared of being the new kid. That making friends isn't a strength of mine, and I'm destined to be that kid who walks swiftly through the hallways, clutching my backpack straps and staring at the floor, hoping I don't make eye contact with someone with anger management issues. So I didn't say any of that. "You're right. I think it's just the first-day jitters, y'know?"

Zoe's eyes sparkled. She didn't have a clue. "Welcome to the club. We've *all* got the first-day jitters. My dad always says the pool is coldest when you first touch the water so the best thing to do is dive right in."

I wasn't sure what my cousin was trying to say. So I replied with, "Wise words."

Zoe looked off to her left and noticed a boy standing alone. "That's Wyatt. He's never really talked to anyone here. He keeps to himself—always has. Which is why he probably doesn't have any friends."

Wyatt was short. He had wavy black hair and a pale complexion that would make a vampire jealous. He kind of looked like a porcelain doll. "Has anyone tried to be *his* friend?"

"Actually, yes. *I* tried talking to him last year, but he wouldn't hear any of it," she sighed. "He was a *jerk* to me."

"Why are you telling me this?" I asked.

Zoe glanced at me. "Because I don't want you to be like him."

My smile tightened. When I looked back at Wyatt, he was gone.

"So have you raised any money yet for the food drive?" Zoe asked out of nowhere.

"Food drive?" I asked. "I haven't heard of anything about that."

"They sent pamphlets to all of the student's houses last week," she said. "Oh, that's right . . . you just moved into your new place, didn't you?"

I nodded.

"Well, it's probably somewhere at your house. We're supposed to raise money by selling fruit or something. I'm already up to ten boxes sold."

"Is there a prize or anything?" I asked. Normally these kinds of things had cool prizes—ray guns and little helicopters and stuff.

"Not a prize for one person, but if the school collectively raises over ten grand, we get to take a trip the week before school is out."

"Where to?"

Zoe shrugged her shoulders. "Does it matter? Anything to get out of school for a day."

I smiled at my cousin. She was actually a little cooler than I thought.

Mr. Cooper opened the side door to the gymnasium. Thank goodness, too, because Zoe's conversation was making me feel a little edgy. He stepped outside and held the door open with his foot, ushering the rest of us to exit the gym for some "productive activity" outside. Great, just what I needed. Exercise.

Outside, the students were given a few different options. Since it was the first day of school, Mr. Cooper apparently thought the best thing to do was take it lightly and allow kids to choose what sport they wanted to play. Some played football. Only a couple played basketball. The rest of them, like me, chose to walk laps around the track. It was the easiest option that didn't require choosing teams or working up a sweat.

I could tell Zoe wanted to play football with a few of her friends, but she decided to walk the track by my side. It wasn't a huge sacrifice for her, but I appreciated it. A little goes a long way with me.

"So what do you want to know?" she asked.

I didn't understand her question. "What do you mean?"

"About this school. What do you want to know about this school? I imagine most schools are the same, but there's gotta be a *couple* differences here and there. What'd you do at your old school?"

I thought about it for a moment. "I didn't do much. I was in the art club, but that's about it."

"That's fun," Zoe said as she started skipping along the track.

Zoe reminded me of my sister, Lucy, who was also somewhere in the building, adjusting to life as a new student. To be fair, it was far easier for her since she was in third grade. Most third graders barely even know they exist. They haven't become "self-aware" yet—like artificial intelligence that hasn't realized it has an identity.

Zoe spoke in an excited manner, which was surprisingly contagious. "There's a *ton* of stuff to do here. Not a lot of schools have as much as us. Buchanan actually prides itself on how huge of a selection we have. There's all kinds of sports teams, different groups, and a bunch of random clubs you can join. I'm sure there's an art club somewhere around here. I'll help you find it."

I nodded my head but was distracted by some movement out of the corner of my eye. It was the edge of the track where the tree line was the thickest. I stopped in place and stared for a second to see if anything moved again, but nothing did.

"What is it?" Zoe asked.

I kept staring into the dense foliage. It was just a mess of green leaves and heavy shadows—except for a pair of the whitest eyes I'd ever seen. I froze in place and rubbed my eyes. Was I seeing things straight or was it part of the "first-day jitters" that Zoe and I had spoken about?

When I looked again, they were gone.

"I guess I just . . . " I stopped talking when I looked at Zoe's face.

Zoe was standing behind me with her eyes peeled wide open, staring into the same spot in the tree line that I had been studying only seconds ago. "Did you see that?" she asked.

A chill ran down my spine. "I did. Do you know what it was?"

She shook her head and started walking along the track again. "Come on. Let's get out of here. I think I'd rather *not* get eaten by a creature in the woods today."

I knew it wasn't a monster we had seen. I'm not that into scary stories and watch enough with my dad to know monsters are fake . . . at least I *think* they're fake. At that moment, I didn't feel the need to test that theory, so I caught up with Zoe and we spent the rest of class making jokes to distract ourselves from whatever it was that had spied on us.

Little did I know it was the first time I'd ever seen a ninja. I'd do anything to take that moment back and just keep walking. Of course, that's not how it turned out, and my curiosity got the better of me.

Tuesday. 10:30 a.m. Gym class.

The next day, Mr. Cooper took attendance as he had before. I was surprised he remembered who I was. As he approached me, he said my name and checked me off the list.

Zoe hadn't left the girl's locker room yet, so I was stuck in the gymnasium standing by myself. I pushed my hands into my pockets and watched the other kids laugh and make jokes with each other before the class officially started. A couple of them even glanced in my direction. I didn't hear what they said, but I'm pretty sure it was about me.

"Hey, *new* kid," said a voice from behind me.

I turned around and was met by a taller student. He was very plain looking with slicked back brown hair. It's possible that it was greasy, but it's also possible he just used way too much gel. "Me?" I asked.

The brown-haired boy outstretched his arms. "I don't see any other *new* kids around here, do you?"

I glanced around. "Uh, I guess I wouldn't know."

"Of course not," he said as he held out his hand. "My name's Brayden, and *you* just passed my *test*."

I shook his cold clammy hand. It was gross and I had to very consciously decide not to rip my hand away from his in disgust. It was my second day of school! I didn't want to embarrass anyone . . . *yet*. "My name's Chase. Chase Cooper. What test did I just pass?"

Brayden shrugged his shoulders. "I don't know. It's just an icebreaker. Y'know, something to break . . . the *ice*."

Smart one, this kid. "Nice to meet you."

"Pleased to meet *you*, Chase. So how was your first day of class yesterday?"

"It was all right," I answered. As I blinked, I hoped he couldn't read my thoughts. *Please just walk away. You're weird and sweaty.*

"Huh," Brayden grunted as he crossed his arms. He remained in place like a statue.

What did this kid want me to say? That it was an epic first day? That it was lame? Whatever it was, I guess I didn't care, because I didn't try to keep the conversation going. We stood there in an awkward silence, occasionally making eye contact, wondering who the next to speak would be.

"Chase," Zoe called from nearby. "Come on, let's walk the track again."

I glanced at Brayden. He still didn't say anything. He just stood there looking sad. Being the nice guy I am, I couldn't just walk away from him. "You want to join us?"

Brayden's face slowly cracked open a smile. It was one of the scariest things I'd seen in my life. "Sure!" he said.

Zoe was nice about it. She seemed to know Brayden from previous years at this school. "Hi, Brayden. Find any werewolves lately?"

"No, but it's not for lack of trying," Brayden answered.

Suddenly, Brayden seemed a little more interesting to me. "You look for werewolves?"

"*Hunt* werewolves," he said sharply. "I *hunt* werewolves."

Yeah, this kid was cool. "Ever find any?" I asked.

"Never," he replied. "Not a one."

"Maybe someday," I said. It was pretty unlikely that this dude was going to catch a werewolf, but who was I to shatter his dreams? "Just keep trying, I guess."

As we stepped out of the gym doors, the sun poured across the school parking lot like a hot wet blanket. It was muggy and awful outside. Zoe immediately started flapping the bottom of her tank top.

"Oh, gross," she said. "Great. Everyone's gonna sweat and stink for the rest of the day. That's so nasty."

I laughed. When she said it like that, it *did* seem nasty. Zoe was always the cleanest one at family events, always washing her hands and wiping her face.

As we walked the path to the track, Brayden was talking about his love of werewolves. At first it was great, but it got boring really fast. He just kept repeating the same things over and over about how real werewolves live in Wisconsin or something. This boy would *not* shut his mouth.

Zoe was good at pretending to care, though I know she actually didn't. Seeing her smile and nod, I realized how obvious it actually was and wondered if she had ever done that to me. Didn't matter— we hardly talked outside of school.

"So that's why a lot of people think werewolves actually come from *Wisconsin*," Brayden said, breathing heavily.

"That's *neat*!" Zoe said, almost convincingly.

"What happens if you ever find one?" I asked.

Brayden paused. "Of course, I want to find one someday, but at the same time, I hope I never do. If I ever get close enough to one, I'll probably snap a picture with my camera. That is, if I have my camera on me."

Zoe started glancing at the tree line again as soon as we arrived at the track. There were several other students in front of us with even more trailing behind. I knew she was looking for those eyes from yesterday. What could they have possibly been? And then I glanced at Brayden . . .

"Hey," I said to him. "Have you ever heard any stories of anything living in *these* woods?"

Zoe's attention snapped at me. Her brow was furrowed and if she could have stared daggers into my soul, she totally would have.

"In *these* woods?" Brayden asked as he looked at the trees. "I've never heard anything strange about them. Why? Did you see something?"

Zoe's glare warned me not to mention anything, but she's family—she'll forgive me. "I saw a set of eyes watching me yesterday. Zoe saw them too."

"*Why* would you say anything?" Zoe asked. She looked at Brayden. "If you tell *anyone* about this, just say it was *Chase* that saw something, okay? I don't need this kind of paranoid delusion following me into middle school next year."

Brayden scratched his head. "You two saw someone watching you from the trees? What color were the eyes?"

"Blue," I answered. At least I *remembered* them being blue.

Brayden scratched at his rough chin. "Y'know . . . I've heard stories . . . no. There's no way."

Suddenly Zoe was interested. All this "cool girl" talk disappears when you put a real mystery in front of her face. "There's no way, what? What were you *going* to say?"

Brayden stepped closer to the tree line. Naturally, Zoe and I followed. As he leaned into the shadows, he mumbled some stuff to himself, but I couldn't understand what he was saying. It was strange . . . it sounded as if he said . . . *ninjas.*

And then he reached his hand into the woods. I knew what was about to happen next because it happens in movies all the time. The innocent doofus reaches his hand into a dark area and loses it.

"Wait!" I shouted, but it was too late.

Brayden was suddenly yanked into the trees. In a rush of activity, he disappeared. It looked as if shadows came to life and swallowed him up. I'd just met this kid and I already regretted it.

Zoe cupped her hand over her mouth, muffling a scream I knew would come out sooner or later. Without thinking (I seem to be guilty of this a lot), I jumped into the woods to chase after Brayden.

"No!" Zoe yelled.

As soon as I planted my feet into the ground beyond the border of the woods, I clenched my eyes tight, afraid of what kind of monsters I would be face to face with. Was Brayden's theory of werewolves correct? Was one going to be standing there with a half-eaten boy in its jaws? I forced my eyes open.

Nothing.

The area was empty. There were no monsters, no people, and no Brayden. I scanned farther through the trees, focusing on seeing any kind of movement against the still areas, but there was nothing.

At that moment, the branches shook from behind me. I thought my heart was going to explode as I flipped around to face my attacker. In all the chaos, I forgot that Zoe was even with me. Weird, because less than ten seconds had passed since I'd jumped into the woods.

"Where's Brayden?" Zoe whispered.

"I don't know," I answered. "And I can't even tell where they took him!"

"Who's *they*?"

I shrugged my shoulders. "Werewolves, I guess? Maybe they've finally gotten fed up with his terrible hunting skills and have taken action into their own paws. Get it? Paws?" It was a terrible joke, but hopefully it helped Zoe feel better.

She laughed. "Human hunters," she sneered. "Too bad they picked the strangest kid to kidnap and study, right? Look at the ground."

I did, but couldn't see what she was talking about. It was just moist dirt, or *mud,* as a scientist would probably call it. "What about it?"

"There's no tracks," Zoe said. "It doesn't even look like there are tracks from *Brayden.* Whatever yanked him in here *had* to have struggled with him, right?"

"Yeah," I said. "I don't think Brayden would've gone willingly. And there wouldn't have been enough time to cover any tracks because I followed him in here almost immediately."

"What did you see right after you stepped through the trees?"

Another chill ran down my spine. "*Nothing.* There was *nothing* back here. No signs of anything that would've grabbed him, and even stranger, no sign of Brayden himself."

Zoe folded her arms and made the "smartie-pants" face I hate. "You know what I'm wondering?"

I sighed. "Do tell."

"I'm wondering why we don't just go straight to the coach with this. Why follow Brayden in here? It's counterproductive. Mr. Cooper would probably get the police and Brayden would be found in an instant."

"Unless it was *werewolves*," whispered a voice from above.

My body froze as I stared at my cousin. She was staring right back at me with her eyes as wide as I'd ever seen on a person that wasn't a cartoon. For a split second, I wanted to warn her that they'd fall out of her head. She'd probably slap my arm for being hilarious at an inappropriate time.

I looked up in the trees and was surprised by what I saw. *Nothing again.* A whole lot of nothing happening out there today.

"Right here, buck-o," whispered the voice again, this time from in front of Zoe and me.

When I turned, I saw not only one kid standing in front of us, but several. There must've been fifteen or twenty of them, all dressed in the same black uniforms. Their faces were covered with masks that only showed their eyes. There was no way this was happening, right? These kinds of things only happen in movies, and mostly movies from the eighties! My *dad's* movies.

"Are you . . . " I started asking.

"*Ninjas*," said the kid in the mask. The rest of the ninjas behind him punched their chests once and let out a "ha!" sound at the same time. I couldn't help but chuckle at how choreographed it was.

"What's so funny?" asked the ninja. "You *dare* laugh at us?"

"Not at *you*," I said. "Just at the fact that it all sounded like you were gonna laugh at the same time but stopped instead. Plus, you're a bunch of kids out here wearing pajamas and hiding in the woods.

If *that's* not a red flag for a guidance counselor, I don't know what is. Besides, you guys aren't very good since you're all standing here in front of us right now. Aren't ninjas supposed to be a secret?"

The ninja stepped forward, revealing Brayden standing behind him. "We've taken your friend prisoner because he got too close to our operation. We've revealed ourselves to *you* because there was a possibility you'd seek help from Mr. Cooper. We've come too far as a clan and can't let it all fizzle out because of a tattle-tale."

"Are you all right?" Zoe asked Brayden.

Brayden nodded but didn't say anything.

The first ninja spoke again. "We'll release him to you under one condition."

What a strange school. I've been here one day, and I've already met a clan of secret ninjas that's holding a kid I just met hostage. How valuable was Brayden to me? Not very. I only just met the boy, but again, being the nice guy I am . . . "Name it."

"You walk out of these woods and tell no one what you saw today," said the ninja.

"But master," said one of the ninjas from the back. I was surprised because it was a girl's voice. "They've seen too much! We cannot let them leave here!"

The first ninja raised his fist in the air. The girl quickly bowed out of respect and stepped back in line. This kid had power, I'll admit that.

"Fine," I said as I glanced at my cousin.

"Deal," said Zoe.

They released Brayden. He stumbled toward us with his hands behind his back. In the short amount of time they had him, they had already tied his hands together. Maybe they were better than I thought.

At that moment, I heard the air horn Mr. Cooper used to signal when there was five minutes left of class. It was his way of lazily telling us to return to the gym. Zoe, Brayden, and I turned toward the school.

When I looked back, the ninjas were gone without a trace.

Wednesday. 7:45 a.m. Homeroom.

Buchanan School started sixth graders on a schedule similar to middle school so the transfer next year wouldn't be as shocking. It was cool because we were the only kids in the school with this type of schedule. I guess every day was going to start with a fifteen-minute homeroom, where we'd all gather our things together and take attendance. Another cool thing about it was no assigned seating. Students were allowed to sit wherever they wanted.

I was the last in the room just before the bell rang.

"Cutting it close, aren't you?" Zoe asked as she unzipped her backpack. It was bright red with speckled straps. There was a small plastic sleeve on the side that had her name written on it. She made a smiley face with the "o."

I smiled and mocked her. "*You're* cutting it close."

"That doesn't even make sense," she replied.

"Think about it for a minute, and it *will*," I said.

Zoe's eyes darted back and forth and the gears in her head clearly cranked. In the time it took her to think, I sat in the seat behind her. Finally, she turned around.

"I still don't get it," she said.

Poor Zoe. *That* was the joke, but I didn't have the heart to tell her. "Never mind."

Homeroom went on as the teacher made the announcements for the day. I zoned out watching the clock as the sound of their voice trailed over my head, speaking about football tryouts, the school lunch menu, and other dumb things that didn't concern me. Something about the food drive and how it was only the third day of school and we were a quarter of the way to our goal. I thought I should probably find that thing the school mailed to my house.

As I envisioned the teacher's words floating over my head, I started to see myself floating there as well. I drifted over the other students, free from this horrible place called "school." And then I flipped my body over and saw the clouds over my head. They were white and fluffy, like marshmallows. I positioned my legs to point at the floor and zoomed—

"*Hey*," Zoe's voice said, interrupting my awesome daydream. "You comin' or what?"

I had a way of losing track of reality when I daydreamed. If I were in a job interview, I'd probably try to hide that fact when they asked about my weaknesses. And also my allergy to bees. ADHD and bees are my weaknesses.

Zoe was standing over my desk waiting for me. The other students had already left the room. Man, I must've been *completely* out of it.

"Sorry." I stood from my desk and watched a folded sheet of paper fall to the floor. Someone had wedged it under my forearm when I wasn't paying attention.

"A secret admirer?" Zoe asked. "Already? Chase, you move too quickly for your own good."

I gestured to my scrawny body. "What girl *wouldn't* want this?"

Zoe laughed. It made me feel better.

"What's it say?" Zoe asked.

I unfolded the sheet of paper and read the writing.

Chase,

Be at the edge of the woods today at the start of gym class. Bring your cousin. Cookies and soda will be provided.

There was no signature.

"Cookies and soda?" Zoe asked.

Great. I'd read the note out loud without meaning to. My dad would always make fun of me because I whispered anything I ever read, even if I meant to read it in my head. "Mouth breather," is what he'd call me. It was in good fun, but it got annoying sometimes.

"The ninjas want us to return?" Zoe asked. "And they're offering soda and cookies as bait? Are they serious? Has anything else in the history of traps ever screamed '*Trap!*' so loudly?"

"It doesn't say it was from the ninjas," I said. "Maybe it's from Brayden."

"The werewolf boy? Yeah, right. Like he'd be smart enough to pull off a trap like this . . . actually, maybe you *are* right. It's such an obvious scheme that I wouldn't be surprised if it *was* him."

Glancing at the clock, I saw that it was only a little after eight in the morning. Gym wasn't for another two and a half hours. Wonderful. I can't stand waiting for the microwave to beep after a *minute*. How was I going to last two and a half *hours*?

Wednesday. 10:40 a.m. Gym class.

By this time, my hands were shaking. I had endured two different classes in anticipation of gym. At one point in the morning, I had even worked up a cold sweat. Zoe made fun of me the whole time.

She was right behind me when I entered the woods again at the same place as the day before. I clenched my jaw as I stepped foot into the moist dirt, or *mud*, waiting to get punched in the face. Luckily that never happened.

Instead, we were met right away by one of the ninjas. He was alone, carrying a zip-locked baggie of Oreo cookies and two orange sodas. In my entire life, I can honestly say I never expected a ninja to greet me with cookies and drinks. It was weird.

"What's this about?" I asked.

"You'll see soon enough," the ninja whispered. "Eat your cookies and follow me."

Now, I know I should be cautious when given snacks by a shady character, but c'mon . . . they were *Oreo cookies*! Did I mention they were *double-stuffed*? I think even the best of us have our weaknesses.

"Lead the way," I said, grabbing the baggie of cookies.

"You're seriously going to eat those?" Zoe asked as she followed behind.

"Darn right."

Zoe smirked. "Good. 'Cause I didn't want to be the only one eating them. Gimme some."

I took a cookie from the baggie and handed it to her. The ninja in front of us wasn't walking very quickly. Maybe he wasn't in as much of a hurry as we were, but gym class was only fifty minutes long, and twenty minutes had already passed.

"Stop," the ninja said. And then he turned around to face us again. "We're here."

Without moving my head, I glanced around the area in front of us. "So we only walked about ten steps, and now we're in your secret hideout? There's no one here. What gives?"

The ninja didn't answer. He slowly lifted his hand up, pointing at something behind us. When I turned around, I saw what he was pointing at.

Zoe and I had only walked about ten feet. We were only about fourteen feet from the edges of the woods that we entered. But in the amount of time it took us to walk this far, the entire clan of ninjas had quietly entered the area. They stood like charcoal-colored statues facing us.

"Man, these guys are *good*," I whispered.

"They're *all right*," Zoe said.

The ninja at the front of the group approached us. I couldn't be sure, but I thought it was the same one from the day before. As I studied his movement, I kind of thought he looked like a "mini-ninja." Y'know, almost like a toy. This thought caused me to chuckle again.

"What's so funny?" the ninja asked. He even had a high-pitched voice. It *wasn't* the ninja from the day before.

"It's nothing. I just—"

"Do you know why you're here?" the ninja asked, interrupting me.

I pulled the note from my gym shorts. I had been anxious all day about this meeting, which meant that I'd opened and closed the note about a hundred times, reading and re-reading it. The sheet of paper was falling apart as I held it out to the masked boy. "I got this in homeroom."

The ninja shook his small head. "You're here because we've *allowed* you to be. You've been invited to join our clan. It's not an invitation you should take light—"

This time, *I* interrupted him. "*Yes*. Yes, yes, and yes please, with a side of French onion *yes*."

The ninja paused. "You haven't even heard our proposal yet."

"I don't care," I replied. "Ninjas are the coolest thing since wireless video game controllers. Of course I want to be a ninja!"

Zoe folded her arms and grumbled.

The short kid looked at her. "The invitation is for *you* as well, darling."

"Ew," Zoe said. "*Don't* call me darling."

"Apologies," the ninja said. "Your cousin has just decided to join our clan. What says you?"

"Meh," Zoe said. "Is this whole thing a secret?"

The ninja nodded like a bobble-head toy. Seriously, he looked like a stinkin' child's plaything!

"So nobody will ever know I was in this club?" Zoe asked.

"Correct."

After a sigh, she looked at me and tightened her lips. "Why not? Sounds like fun."

"Excellent!" shouted the ninja. The minions behind him raised their arms in the air and made the same "*ha*" sound as the day before. The ninja turned around but glanced over his shoulder at us. "Be here tomorrow at this time. If you wish to join our clan, each of you must find a four-leaf·clover and present it to us in this spot."

"Wait," I said. "We're not automatically entered into your little ninja gang?"

The boy nodded. I could tell from his squinty eyes that he was smiling under the mask. And then he spoke loudly. "Ninja *vanish*!"

Immediately, two ninjas hopped down from the treetops and started clapping chalkboard erasers together violently in front of my face. White powder exploded into the air, making it impossible to see anything. When the smoke cleared, the ninjas were gone.

"Amazing," I whispered.

"A little dorky," Zoe snipped quietly.

"Then why'd you say you'd join?"

Zoe's shoulders slumped down, and she waved her arms out. "Because you're *new* at this school, and I want you to feel normal about it. I don't know what it's like being the new kid, but I'm sure it *stinks*. If joining a ninja clan will help you get on your feet, then by golly, *that's* what I'll do." She paused. "*What a weird sentence I just spoke!* I do it 'cause you're family, y'know. You're cool enough,

Chase, but if it takes a little bit of a push, then *I'll* be the one to push."

I smiled at the sappy way she was telling me she cared. "Gross, stop it already. You're gonna bore me to the point of comatose."

Zoe shook her head, confused. "That's not even a *thing*!"

Thursday. 7:45 a.m. Homeroom.

I took my seat behind Zoe again since the desk was open. She turned around wearing a stupid grin. I knew why she was grinning, and I couldn't help but return the dorky smile.

"Did you find one?" Zoe whispered.

I shook my head. "No. I looked all night in my yard. There were a billion three-leaved clovers, and a couple of two-leaved ones . . . I even found one with five leaves, but none with four. I'll have to spend the first half of gym class with my face buried in the grass looking for one, I guess."

She slammed a textbook down on my desk. It made enough ruckus that the entire class noticed.

"Sorry," she said, embarrassed.

"It's all right," said the homeroom teacher as he continued making the announcements. "And the food drive total is up to over three *thousand* dollars! All the cash and checks are sitting in the front office inside a plastic container for everyone to see. It's quite a spectacle, really. If we can fill two of those containers, we'll have reached our goal of ten thousand dollars! And you know what *that* means . . . "

"*Class trip!*" the students said in unison.

When the teacher started speaking again, Zoe turned around and opened the textbook to a page in the middle. At the center of the page were *two* four-leaf clovers.

I was shocked. I'd used a stinkin' magnifying glass when I searched for over three hours the night before! "How'd you find *two* of them?"

"I found them *years* ago," she whispered. "I've always had them."

"Well, when you show them you have two, they'll probably promote you immediately."

Her jaw dropped and she gasped. "Are you *stupid*? One is for *you*! I brought it in case you couldn't find any!"

Obviously I hoped that was the case, but I hadn't wanted to be rude and *assume* it. I took a clover from the textbook and studied it closely. "Really? That's . . . *awesome*. Thanks!"

"Best cousin ever, right?"

I chuckled.

"You guys are seriously considering joining those ninjas?" Brayden's voice asked.

He was in the seat next to us. Strange that I didn't even notice him until he spoke. Guess he had that kind of a personality.

"Why not?" I asked.

"Because they're ninjas. Ninjas *aren't* good guys," Brayden said, slouching in his seat.

"What're you talkin' about?" I said. Was Brayden really against the whole ninja thing? This from a boy who hunts werewolves and brags about it? "Ninjas are all about honor and helping people. I read all about it on the internet last night," I said, which was true. Sad, isn't it?

And I learned some crazy things! Did you know ninjas were mostly peaceful farmers that lived in the mountains? The reason they were all stealthy is so they could defend themselves when they were outnumbered. A few people bought into the fighting system of ninjutsu and went around assassinating people with their skills. And you know what they say—a few bad apples spoil the bunch.

"No," Brayden said. "*Real* ninjas weren't bad guys by default, but the ninjas *you're* talking about joining . . . *are*."

I shook my head and said the only thing that came to mind. "*Nuh-uh.*"

Thursday. 10:35 a.m. Gym class.

Zoe and I sprinted toward the wooded area on the track as soon as we exited the gymnasium doors. Mr. Cooper had his sunglasses on and was lying back in a reclining lawn chair just to the right of the exit. His air horn was sitting on the ground next to him. It was the fourth day I'd been in this school, and this was the position I was used to seeing him in. Lazy and uncaring. I think I'll be a gym teacher when I get older.

Once we entered the trees, the ninjas were there waiting for us. I guess there wasn't any reason to sneak up or anything, since we had an appointment.

The shortest of the ninjas stepped forward. "I assume you both have your clovers, otherwise it would be pea-brained of you to return here."

At the same time, Zoe and I held out our clovers.

"Excellent," said the ninja. "*Eat* them."

Did he just say what I think he said? Was this kid crazy? But when I looked at Zoe, she was already chewing on hers. There was no way I'd be shown up by my cousin, so I popped the thing into my mouth and started going to town on it. I expected the taste of dirt and grass, but was actually surprised. It wasn't half bad! It was sort of tart and bitter. It's possible that I'd even try it again someday.

"Sick!" the ninja said with a laugh. "I can't believe you guys did that!"

Zoe stopped chewing and looked angry. She spit out the clover and stepped toward the small ninja. "I'm about to make you eat a mouthful of grass, you little—"

The ninja put his hands up, chuckling. "Wait, wait! I'm sorry. It's cool, you guys are in the clan. Seriously, you're *in*."

Zoe perked up. "Really? Because you just made me *eat* a clover."

I don't know why Zoe minded. I was still chewing on mine. "So we're in?"

The ninja pulled the black mask off his face. I gulped the clover down as soon as I recognized the kid—it was Wyatt, the short guy we'd seen standing alone the other day.

"Wyatt?" Zoe asked. "*You're* the ninja leader?"

"I am," he said, nodding. "And the two of you are our newest recruits."

I almost jumped with joy, but I'm not so sure a ninja would hop up and down when they were happy. "*Nice*," I said. "So what's next?"

Wyatt walked past us. The other ninjas remained in place in the woods, watching as he neared the edge and continued speaking. "Now there's just *one* more test to pass."

"But you just said we were in," Zoe grunted with her arms folded. "*In* is *in*, isn't it?"

"Sorta," Wyatt said as he parted some leaves. "But you have to show your allegiance to the clan so that we know you're dead serious."

Oh no. This is what I feared. He was going to have us *kill* someone.

"You must perform a final task," Wyatt said, studying the other students walking the track on the outside of the woods. "One that's *incriminating.*"

"I don't think I can kill anyone," I whispered.

Wyatt looked over his shoulder at me. "Are you *nuts*? *Kill* someone? What's the matter with you?"

I stared at the ground, embarrassed I'd opened my big mouth. As I kicked at the dirt, I whispered, "It was a joke."

Wyatt shook his head in disbelief. "*Doubt* it," he said as he returned his attention to the innocent bystanders walking the track. "There's no killing here. Come on, *we're sixth graders.*"

"Then what is it?" Zoe asked.

Wyatt pointed his finger at one of the girls on the track. She was walking with her friends. A purple and pink purse was slung from her shoulder. "Steal Emily's purse and return it to me within the hour."

Zoe joined Wyatt at his side. "*What*? You want us to steal Emily's purse? Are *you* nuts? We're not stealing anything from anyone! Besides, those girls are my friends!"

Wyatt turned around and looked at me. "Then the two of you are dismissed. Leave this place at once."

I sighed, looking at my cousin. She was standing with her hands on her hips—the usual "you've got to be kidding me" look in her eyes. It's a look I'm familiar with. I didn't want to argue with her, so I didn't, but she must've seen my hesitation.

"Fine," she said softly. She was doing it for me.

"Excellent," said Wyatt as he slipped his mask back on.

"So where's our black pajamas that we wear since we're ninjas?" I asked.

Wyatt shook his head and spoke from behind the fabric on his face. "You get those *after* you return with the purse."

"After?" Zoe asked.

This was going to be more difficult than I thought.

Wyatt and the clan disappeared from behind us. Zoe and I waited until Emily and her friends made a full lap around the track, so they were right in front of us again. I could see her purple purse swinging gently over her shoulder. The strap was short. It wouldn't be as easy as sneaking it off her arm.

"What do you think?" I asked Zoe.

"I think I'm gonna be sick," she replied.

She can be such a drama queen. "Thank you for going along with this."

She rolled her eyes. "Pretty sure I'm already regretting it."

I straightened my posture, feeling guilty about Zoe's involvement. I started to talk, to tell her she could back out of it if she wanted, but she interrupted me.

"Look!" she cried as she pointed. "They're taking a break in the grass! She put her purse on the ground!"

When I looked out, I saw that Zoe was right. Emily was lying on her back. She and her friends were staring at the clouds or something, I couldn't tell exactly what, but I didn't care. The purse was free from her shoulder.

"Follow my lead," Zoe said as she burst through the tree line.

I jumped through, trying to keep up, but she was fast! She sprinted like some kind of gazelle running from a predator! What was she going to do? Was she just going to snatch the purse and run like heck? I'm pretty sure those girls would notice something as obvious as that and, wait a second. Was she going to use *me* as a distraction?

My heart started to race as I saw the whole disaster play out in my head. She would scrape the purse off the ground. Just as the girls would notice, I'd suddenly appear, hobbling like a penguin because I suck at running. In all the chaos, they would see me as the bad guy and since I'm pretty slow, *I'd* be the one those lions would devour. *How could Zoe do such a thing to me?*

I watched as my cousin finally made it to her group of friends. My heart stopped as I waited for her to grab the purse, but to my surprise, she didn't. Instead, she tripped just as she reached the circle and tumbled across the grass violently until finally flopping about ten feet away from them.

And then I realized her brilliance. Zoe's friends dashed to her aid as she clutched at her scraped knees. They were so concerned with her that they left all their belongings behind in the grass. There were shoes with socks stuffed into them, stretchy hair bands, and one lonely purple and pink purse. Emily had left without it.

I grabbed it while watching Zoe and her friends talk in the grass. She glanced over at me and winked. I nodded at her before sprinting back to the woods as quickly as my scrawny legs could carry me.

When I hopped through the trees, Wyatt was waiting for me all by himself. The clan was nowhere to be seen.

"Well done," he said as he held his hands out.

I dropped Emily's purse into his palms. "So that's it?"

His mask moved as he spoke. "That's it."

Suddenly Zoe stepped into the woods and joined us. Her face looked like she had been slapped around by the dirt fairy. Her lip was even bloody. Man, had she gotten into a fight since I last saw her talking to her friends?

"Happy?" she asked.

"Quite," Wyatt answered. His eyes looked piercing from the ninja mask surrounding them. I couldn't wait to get my hands on one! The mask, I mean . . . not his *eyes*. For the record, I had no intention of getting my hands on one of his eyes.

Wyatt opened the purse and dumped the contents onto the ground. Zoe clenched her fists in anger.

"Why would you do that?" she asked. "Why not just take what you want and leave the rest somewhere she could find it?"

Wyatt chuckled. "Because that's silly. The point of stealing it is that it's ours to do what we want with it."

My cousin stared at the short ninja. I thought time had stopped because of how thick the tension was. I was waiting for her to throw a punch at him. She tended to do things like that when she was angry.

"I'm out," she said, raising her palms. "This is making me feel like throwing up."

"You can't just leave now, sweetheart!" Wyatt sneered. "You're a member of the clan and guilty of theft! If you leave, we'll make sure you regret it!"

The rest of the ninja clan stepped out from behind the trees. Many of them pulled their masks back over their faces. Their eyes looked angry.

"Whatever," Zoe said as she stepped through the trees. From the other side of the foliage, she spoke to me. "You comin' or what?"

I looked at Wyatt, who was still holding Emily's purse. The ninja was calmly staring at me, shaking his head slowly. It was one of the hardest things I've said in my life. "Sorry, Zoe. I think I'll stay here."

Friday. 9:30 a.m. Art class.

I got to school late this morning, and it wasn't by accident. All night, my stomach had twisted and turned from not only stealing a girl's purse, but also betraying my own cousin. My parents didn't seem to notice, but my sister sure did. She was nice about it, not by asking what was wrong, but hanging out with me while I wasted time playing video games.

When I woke up, I acted sick. My mom bought it for a little bit, at least enough to let me skip homeroom. But when she caught me playing basketball in the driveway, she took me straight to school. She barely gave me time to get ready! I arrived for second period art class with messed up hair.

When I walked into class, I expected Zoe to scold me, but it was worse than that. She completely *ignored* me. I know she saw me walk into the room—everyone did, and a few kids made fun of my hair. But she just sat at her desk with her watercolors, painting unicorns or something.

When I looked at her canvas, I saw that she was painting flowers. I was wrong about the unicorns.

"Hey," I said.

She didn't answer.

"Hey Chase," said Brayden. The desks in the room were separated into clumps of four. He was in the clump behind Zoe's.

"Hi," I said unenthusiastically.

He switched from his clump of desks to the one Zoe was at. "Did you hear about the food drive money?"

I had only gotten to school, so I hadn't heard about anything yet. "No. What about it?"

"It's *gone*," Brayden said. "The container is completely *empty*."

"What are you talking about? That thing was filled with cash and sitting in the front office! Somebody stole it?"

"Just the money. The container's still there, and nobody knows who did it," Brayden said.

I felt that same sick feeling roll around in my guts. I had to take a seat and breathe slowly through my nose. I didn't know what it meant, but I had my suspicions. And from the looks of it, Zoe did, too.

"Anyway," Brayden continued. "That's that, so you're all caught up in case you see a mountain of cash sitting somewhere."

I watched in silence as he returned to his seat.

"Happy with your new friends?" Zoe asked. She wasn't even trying to hide her sarcasm.

I didn't want to make excuses. "I'm sorry about yesterday. Really."

"*Really?*"

"Really!"

Zoe tapped the water off her paintbrush and set it on a wet paper towel next to her canvas. "So you quit, then, hmm?"

I didn't answer.

"You quit, and you also returned Emily's purse, right?" Zoe asked. Her voice was rising. It grated on me.

"Well, *no*," I whispered.

"Of course not," Zoe said. "You know how I know? Because she called me last night wondering if I had seen it anywhere. You know what I had to do then?"

I took a breath. I remember it being the longest pause in the history of all pauses. "What?"

She leaned over and whispered, "I *lied* to her."

That was it. If she was going to give me a guilt trip, I didn't have to take it. "I didn't *ask* you to lie! You could've told her the truth!"

"That I *helped* you steal it?" she whispered coarsely. "Yeah, right. And commit social suicide? Forever to be branded as a *klepto*?"

"Whatever, Zoe. You knew what you were doing."

I could hear her teeth grinding. "That I was helping my cousin fit in at a new school? That I felt so bad for him because he's such a *dork* that I couldn't stand to watch him be *alone*?"

I nodded my head, destroyed by what she said. "There it is."

"There *what* is?"

"The truth. You've finally revealed how you really feel about it," I said, surprised by the shaking in my own voice. "Well, you don't have to worry about it anymore. I guess I'll leave you alone forever, then. Happy?"

Ah, the classic guilt trip. I was good at those. Now I only had to wait a few seconds for her apology. And in three . . . two . . . one . . .

"*Good*!" she said as she stood from her desk. She stormed up to the art teacher. He handed her a hall pass, and she disappeared out the door.

And there I sat, smug smile on my face, waiting for an apology that wasn't going to be delivered anytime soon.

I'd never felt so stupid in my life.

Friday. 10:35 a.m. Gym class.

I wasn't sure what to do in gym. Zoe had already gathered with her group of friends, which included Emily. They stood just outside the girls' locker room, gossiping and talking loudly to one another.

I was on the other side of the gymnasium, standing alone, until Brayden joined me.

"Where's Zoe?" he asked.

I nodded my head in her direction.

"Oh," he said. "I heard you guys arguing in art class."

Staring at the floor, I made sure not to make eye contact. The fact that he'd heard us talking meant he might have heard about Emily's purse. "What did you hear us say?"

"*Everything*," he sighed.

I took a breath and continued studying the gymnasium floor.

"Kind of shady to steal a girl's purse like that," Brayden said. "Kind of *shadier* to put that pressure on a family member."

I feigned a large smile. "Thaaaaaanks. I'll be sure to remember that next time."

"Told you those were the bad guys," Brayden said.

Would this kid just shut up already? "Look, I'm not arguing with you here. All right? Would you mind walking away?"

Brayden shook his big dumb head and chuckled. Then he pushed himself off the wall and walked toward the gymnasium doors.

I let everyone filter out before exiting. I didn't feel like having anyone walk behind me.

When I reached the track, I waited until the coast was clear before entering the ninjas' secret hideout. Wyatt was already there in full uniform, as were most of the other ninjas. It was strange because they were all lined in a circle. At its center was a ninja uniform, tightly folded and resting on a small wooden table.

"Welcome, brother," Wyatt's voice said from beneath his mask. "You're one of us now."

I won't lie to you—all the guilt I had felt earlier *disappeared*. The sun was pouring in from overhead, slipping through the leaves of trees. The ground twinkled from specks of water left behind from the morning dew and moist air, like diamonds sprinkled around the hideout. The rays of light fell upon the ninja uniform as if God himself had blessed the cotton it was made from. I scratched at my eyebrow to hide a tear that had formed in the side of my eye.

Wyatt put his arm around me. "There's a spot behind those trees for you to change your clothes. Be quick, brother. We have an important task for you when you're ready."

It was everything I could do to keep from squealing like my sister on Christmas. I did my best to answer calmly, but it only came out in a rapid slur. "*SureI'llberightback!*"

The ninja costume fit like a glove, I tell you. It was like a finely tailored suit that a rich gentleman would special order from Europe. When I emerged from behind the trees, many of my ninja brothers and sisters gasped and clapped softly. I made the outfit look *good*. Or scary. It might've been because my overly skinny body made it look like I was the grim reaper. Whatever, though—strike fear into my enemies, right?

Another ninja to the left of me whipped out a couple bags of Oreos, and we continued our celebration with cookies. I don't even care how silly that sounds. Ninjas and cookies are two of the most awesome things on the planet. Of course they'd go great together!

Wyatt sat by my side with a mouthful of cookie. He chewed it sloppily like a dog. "I'm thankful that you've chosen to become a member of my clan."

"Are there other clans?" I asked.

"No," Wyatt said. "Are you ready for the task we've specifically chosen for you?"

I set my Oreos down on the little table. My first job as a ninja, and in a real ninja uniform—*of course* I was ready! "Yes, tell me what I must do."

Wyatt paused. "Are you sure? You wear the uniform now, so you can't reject any kind of duty you're given."

For a second, I imagined he said "doodie," and I laughed. "No, I won't reject anything. Whatever you want from me, consider it done."

Wyatt nodded and made a "tch tch" sound with his cheek. Immediately, one of the other members of the clan tossed a backpack to the ground in front of me. It was bright red with speckled straps.

I studied it for a moment. I had seen a backpack like this before, but where? And then it hit me. I'd seen the same bag sitting by Zoe's desk earlier in the week. This was *Zoe's* backpack.

"Why do you have that?" I asked.

Wyatt shook his head. "Members of my clan don't ask questions when they're given a task, and yours is simple. All you have to do is take this bag to the front office."

"Sneak it in there? You want me to walk through the school wearing this ninja uniform?"

"No," Wyatt said. "That's why it'll be easy. After gym, you'll change into your normal street clothes and simply take this bag to the front desk. You'll deliver it to the principal, and tell them you found it under a bush outside."

I looked at Zoe's backpack. Could it have been a coincidence? Could this just be the same bag that she has? As I scanned the side of it, I saw her name scribbled on the plastic shield, complete with the smiley face in the "o." It was definitely her bag.

"What's inside?" I asked.

"Vengeance," Wyatt said.

"Vengeance? For what?"

Wyatt pulled his mask back and revealed a face filled with anger. "She *rejected* our offer and embarrassed me in front of my clan. That *cannot* go unpunished. *Enough* questions. As a member of this clan, you must deliver this bag to the office and say nothing else of it. Do you understand?"

Reluctantly, I nodded.

"Do *not* open this bag, or you will suffer the same fate as your cousin," Wyatt warned.

There was that same sick feeling in my gut. I almost felt like barfing.

Friday. 11:25 a.m. Between gym class and lunch.

I waited until everyone in gym had returned to the locker rooms before I stepped out of the woods. The other ninjas had changed clothes and returned with the rest of the class. Mr. Cooper wasn't too attentive, so the fact that I wasn't with them slid past him pretty easily.

With Zoe's backpack slung over my shoulder, I started hiking across the track and field. If I went in through the gymnasium doors, I was sure to get caught, so I decided to walk around the school to the entrance near the front offices.

The bag was heavy on my back. Heavier than a normal bag should be anyway. I imagined she had all her textbooks in it, but I knew that wasn't the truth. Why would Wyatt call it "vengeance" if I were simply delivering an item to the lost and found?

My stomach curdled once more, and I couldn't take it. Zoe was my cousin, and even though she hurt my feelings, she was *still* family. I'd already betrayed her once, and I didn't want to do it again.

I set the bag on the sidewalk and stared at it. I didn't want to see what was inside, because whatever it was, it was in there because I'm an *idiot*. It's *my* fault that Zoe was in this mess, and I was prepared to do whatever it took to get her out of it.

My hand shook as I gripped the zipper. The cold piece of metal stung from how tightly I was pinching it. I clenched my jaw and decided to treat the bag like a Band-Aid—rip it open and get it over with.

I jerked my hand into the air, unzipping Zoe's red backpack. The bag lifted off the ground and flipped upside-down. As it landed, hundreds of coins rolled out and lumps of cash fell to the pavement.

"Oh no," I whispered. My knees betrayed me, and I fell to the ground, staring at all the money that spilled from the red bag.

There was a yellow sheet of paper sticking out from under the coins. I could only read part of it, but I knew what it said. When I yanked it free, I found that I was right.

"Student Hunger Drive, Money Donations," was printed in bold black ink on the yellow paper.

The food drive money that was gone missing this morning had somehow found its way into Zoe's backpack. The ninjas had stolen it and were planning on framing her.

This was bad. Not *just* bad, but *epic* bad. Like end-of-the-world bad. Zoe wouldn't just get a slap on the wrist for something like this. She would get expelled. It would be on her permanent record. Her parents would ground her for the rest of her life. My parents would never let us hang out together again! She'd probably grow old and die alone because of the contents of this backpack!

I couldn't take it to the office. Not even if I told them the truth. Because c'mon, a ninja clan in the woods wants to frame a sixth-grade girl because she refused to join? I just *lived* through it, and even *I* don't believe that tale!

I scooped the loose change and clumps of paper money back into Zoe's backpack. I remembered Brayden telling me nearly three grand had been stolen. If you've never held three grand in a backpack, let me tell you right now that it's not very light.

Paranoid, I made sure nobody was outside watching me. If Wyatt was able to steal all this money from the front office, he could easily be spying on me right at that moment.

Friday. 11:35 a.m. Lunch.

I decided against walking through the front doors of the school for obvious reasons. If anyone had stopped to ask what I was doing, I knew I'd buckle and act super suspicious. I guess a backpack with three thousand dollars will do that to ya.

Instead, I walked to the doors of the cafeteria. They were next to the gym doors, so the trek wasn't that far.

The cafeteria was bustling with activity as kids walked to their tables with trays filled with gross food. I could see Zoe at a table with her friends. Emily was right next to her. Brayden was sitting alone at the table nearest the door. I dashed over to his table and took the seat across from him.

He looked up from his tray. "Where's your food?"

I scanned the room for Wyatt. "Not so hungry."

Brayden took a bite of his mashed potatoes. "What's with the backpack?"

"Y'know," I said, still keeping an eye out, "Sometimes I like to just carry my bag around."

I couldn't see Wyatt anywhere.

Brayden pointed his fork at the bag. "That's not your bag, dummy," he said through a mouthful of food. "That's Zoe's."

"What?" I asked, shocked. "Did I grab the wrong bag again? How silly of me."

"Shut up," Brayden said with a hint of anger in his voice. "You have it on purpose. What's your deal, Chase?"

I glanced at the werewolf hunter across the table as he took a drink from his milk carton. His eyes were soft and doughy. Could he be trusted? We'll see. "This bag is filled with the money from the food drive."

Brayden spit out his milk, spraying it across the table and my face. He punched at his chest as he coughed out the words, "Are you serious?"

I wiped the milk off my cheeks. "Yes! Keep it down, will ya?"

He leaned over. "*Did you steal that money?*" he whispered.

"*No!* But I have it now," I replied. "This is Zoe's bag, and I'm supposed to take it to the office! Wyatt wants to frame her for stealing the money so she'll get in trouble!"

"In trouble is what she'll *wish* she got in! More than likely she'll get in *dead meat*!"

"I know!" I said. "And I don't know what to do!"

Brayden looked over his shoulder, I think to make sure no one was listening in on our conversation. "You need to get that cash back into the container in the office."

"Of course that's what I'd *love* to do, but I doubt it's as easy as walking it in there!" I said loudly. Luckily the students in the cafeteria were louder.

Brayden leaned back in his chair and pried open his milk carton. He took a sip, then set the drink back down on his tray. Then, with a milk mustache, he said, "I'll provide the distraction. No worries there. We'll do it after I finish my food."

"I hope you know what you're doing," I said, feeling a glimmer of hope for the first time since finding the money.

He nodded as he finished his meal. Yeah, it was the weirdest thing. He just kept on nodding while eating his food, but was I going to say anything about it? Nope, because he was going to *help* me. Brayden had moved up on the ladder from a person I hardly knew to a true friend.

Friday. 11:45 a.m. In the hallway during lunch.

Brayden led the way. He was keeping an eye out for anyone in front of us while I made sure nobody was behind. Zoe's red backpack was getting heavier on my shoulder, and I couldn't wait to get rid of the darn thing.

"It's right around this corner," said Brayden. Good thing, too, because being the new kid in school, I hardly knew my way around.

"What's the plan?" I asked.

Brayden poked his head around the corner and glanced through the windows of the front office. "Not sure yet."

The front office was separated by a large counter that was as high as my neck. Behind the counter were several desks where adults stared blankly at their computer monitors. One of the adults was the secretary. I think she stayed in the office the entire day, so I'm at sea about how Wyatt managed to steal the money in the first place. Like I said before, he must've been *good*.

"There are three people working at their desks," said Brayden. "I think if I make enough noise and run down the hallway, they'll probably chase me."

I shook my head. "That won't work. Only *one* of them will chase after you, if even *that*. More than likely, they'll page the security guard to come after you. We have to think of something else."

And then came a familiar voice from behind us. "You could drop the bag off as I instructed you to."

I could tell it was Wyatt. When I turned around, he was standing with his arms at his sides and a scowl across his face. Outside of his ninja outfit, he looked like any other short kid in the school. Average. Forgettable.

Behind him were several other students I didn't recognize, but from how they were standing, it was clear that it was the rest of the clan.

"I can't do that," I said as I pulled Zoe's backpack tighter on my shoulders.

"You don't really have a choice, do you?" Wyatt asked with an ugly smirk.

"Oh, but I think I do," I replied. "You see, *I'm* the one with the bag and the money. Not you."

Wyatt chuckled, as did the rest of the clan behind him. "You're only delaying the inevitable. This can go down in two ways—you can dump the bag in the office, telling them what I told you to say, or you can get caught out here with a backpack full of three grand. Pretty sure they won't believe any story you tell them about me. After all, I'm just an average Joe at this school. I barely have any friends, right?"

The ninja leader was right. If I choose one path, then *Zoe* gets busted. If I wait too long, a teacher will eventually come along, and then *I'll* get busted. That'd be a great way to start a new school, huh? Get caught stealing money from hungry kids. Either way, Wyatt wins.

I had to do something to upset his plan and flip it over on him. I thought frantically about what to do. I looked at Brayden, hoping he would have a suggestion, but he only shrugged his shoulders.

"You're running out of time, Chase," Wyatt sneered.

"Chase?" said a girl's voice. When I looked over, I saw Zoe walking with her friends. *Of course* they'd show up at this exact moment. Isn't that my luck?

"Hey, Zoe," I said, staring at the floor.

"Why do you have my backpack?" she asked, growing visibly upset. "Oh I get it, you were probably instructed to steal *my* stuff too, weren't you?"

Emily spoke up this time. "*Too*? Did your cousin steal my purse?"

I could feel my face getting hotter at the embarrassment. I was about to answer before Zoe spoke again. "Yes, as a matter of fact, he *did*."

"Not without a special someone's help," Wyatt laughed.

Zoe turned around and did what should've been done right after the incident. "Emily, I'm sorry, but I helped my cousin take your purse during gym class yesterday."

The hallway was so quiet I swear I heard a cricket somewhere, *dying* of quietness. Emily's jaw dropped. "But why?"

My cousin paused. "Because I was stupid. I thought helping Chase would get him some friends. I mean, *look* at him and how *pathetic* he is!"

"Thanks," I murmured.

Zoe sighed. "Whatever was in your purse, I promise I'll return to you. Honestly, I will. I'm just so sorry that it even happened."

Emily finally closed her mouth and gulped. And then the most awesome thing happened. She smiled. "It's okay. No big deal. That was my *gym class* purse. All I keep in there is a spare stick of deodorant and a couple quarters for a soda after class."

Zoe's face lit up as if a dark shroud was lifted from it. "I owe you a bunch of quarters then!"

Emily laughed. "Nah, don't worry about it. You did it 'cause you care about your cousin. It was worth it, right?"

I wish I had friends as cool as that.

Wyatt clenched his fists. "It doesn't matter anyway, since you're stuck here with a bag fulla money!"

"A bag full of money?" Zoe asked. "Does my backpack have money in it?"

I couldn't answer, but Zoe could read me like a book. "The money from the food drive . . . it's all in there, isn't it?"

I nodded as Wyatt laughed. His ninja minions laughed along with him, which made the hallway echo with villainous guffawing. If this didn't attract any teachers, I don't know what would.

I did the only thing I could think of. I let the backpack fall into my hands and whipped it at Wyatt as hard as I could to shut him up. Distracted by his own moment of glory, he didn't see the bag coming, and it hit him straight in the face.

The bag burst open. Loose change and tightly wound balls of cash fell to the floor, amidst the sound of gasping students.

With a loud cry, Wyatt tumbled backward into the members of his ninja clan. The students caught him and pushed him back to his feet, whispering quickly among themselves.

And this is the part where things went a little blurry.

Embarrassed, Wyatt threw a punch that landed solidly on my chin. A shock of pain blasted through my body and everything went bright white for a second. The next thing I knew I was on the floor of the hallway, surrounded by a circle of kids yelling something about a fight.

I felt a sharp pain from my lip. As I stood up, I rubbed my fingers across my mouth. Wyatt's punch must've busted my lip open. Blood was all over my fingertips. All I wanted to do was punch him back. Everything inside me boiled with anger and suddenly, the entire world was painted red.

I spat on the floor and saw Zoe's backpack lying next to me. She was also standing in the crowd of shouting students, but she was standing perfectly still. She looked sad.

I glanced back at Wyatt as he landed another punch right into my gut. I clutched at my stomach, afraid I might puke.

I was the new kid at the school. Scrawny and dorky. And I was getting my butt kicked in front of everyone. Wyatt was going to win no matter how hard I fought back. So I did the opposite of what I wanted to do . . .

I decided to let him win.

Standing again, I looked at him. He was bouncing around like some kind of karate master with his hands in the air, waving them back and forth in front of his body. I smiled because it looked like he was playing with one of those puppets attached to strings . . . what are they called? Oh yeah, *marionettes.*

Another punch from Wyatt met with my cheek this time. I'd seen it coming but didn't even try to block it. Why bother? Everything was my fault anyhow, so maybe I deserved a proper beating.

And then the crowd started to calm down a little. Wyatt kept dancing and breathing heavily, occasionally letting out a "whaaaaaaaa," like Bruce Lee in those old movies. He was so engulfed in the moment that he didn't even realize everyone had stopped cheering.

Suddenly I realized what was happening. Somehow in this moment, I had become the bigger man. By refusing to fight back, I was taking a stand of my own. I was standing up to a filthy rotten bully. And it gave me strength.

He threw a kick into the air. Punches are one thing, but getting kicked is a whole other level of "ouch." His foot landed on my arm and a scorching pain shot down my spine. I wasn't sure how much more I could take of this, but I returned to my position in front of him.

"Fight back!" Wyatt yelled. The frustration in his voice was clear.

He swung a right hook at me, but this time I dodged it by leaning backward. "I won't. You're not worth it. If I fight, then *you* win. If I turn in this bag to the office, *you* win. If I get caught with it, *you* win. The only way for me to stop this is if I refuse to play along with your manipulative games. All I should've done was walk away from the beginning, but I can't do that now, can I? I'm stuck here, so the best thing to do is to refuse to fight back."

From the corner of my eye, I could see Zoe smile at me. It was a proud smile.

"Hit me!" Wyatt screamed again as he threw another hook.

I dodged it like before.

One of his ninja minions put their hand on his shoulder. "Come on, man. This is getting weird. Let's just get outta here."

Several of the other ninjas agreed.

Wyatt swung around and slapped the kid in the face. "Don't tell me what to do! And don't you *ever* touch me!"

The ninja leader flung his arm around behind him, swinging wide. It moved too quickly for me to back away from. All I could do was flinch.

But the punch never landed. I pried my eyes open and saw a furious Mr. Cooper dragging Wyatt away from me. The circle of students filled the entire hallway.

"*He* started it!" Wyatt shouted as he kicked his feet. "I caught him with the stolen money! Look at it! It all came pouring out of that red backpack!"

Mr. Cooper released Wyatt's arm and stepped forward, staring at the cash on the floor.

Everyone in the hallway was silent, which made it easy for Wyatt to keep shouting. "That's Zoe's bag! They were in on it together! They *both* stole the money, and I caught them! When I confronted him, he started fighting me! I *had* to defend myself!"

Mr. Cooper pushed the change around with his foot until he saw the yellow sheet of paper that labeled it the food drive money. He glanced around at the students in the hallway. By this time, several of the other teachers had joined, trying to push the kids away from the dropped cash.

"Who's responsible for this?" Mr. Cooper asked.

"I already said *they* were!" Wyatt screamed, pointing at my cousin and me.

Mr. Cooper raised his hand to Wyatt, instructing him to be silent. "I didn't ask *you*, I asked *them*," he said, gesturing to everyone in the hallway.

There was no way any of Wyatt's ninja clan would fess up to it, and if they did, who would believe them? And none of the other kids knew about Wyatt's plan, so all they were good for was shoulders to shrug. The backpack was Zoe's, there was no doubt about that. When they got around to asking why the money was in it, she would claim it was stolen. I doubt she would say anything about the ninjas, but even if she did, who in the world would believe her?

I looked at my cousin. She had a worried look on her face as she glanced back. It looked like there were tears forming in her eyes. She was family, but more importantly, she was a friend.

When Zoe was questioned about Emily's stolen purse, she immediately admitted her foul-up. I took that as a lesson in integrity.

I nodded at Zoe, and then I spoke. "*I* took the money."

Strangely, it was the ninja clan that gasped loudest.

"I *told* you!" Wyatt said, slapping his hands together.

"No, *I* took the money," Brayden suddenly shouted as he stepped forward.

Wait, what? Why did Brayden just say that?

"No! *I* took it!" Zoe shouted.

And then another weird thing happened—other students started stepping forward, confessing that they had stolen the food drive money.

"*I* did it," said a short girl with red hair. She was cute, but that's beside the point.

"It was *me*," said one of the taller students.

"*I* took the money," said yet another.

I watched as several of the ninjas stepped forward and did the same. I can't imagine Wyatt was too happy that they were doing it.

Wyatt's face grew bright red as he clenched his fists again. "*They* took the money!" he screamed as he jumped at me.

Mr. Cooper caught the ninja leader by his collar, pulled him back, then pushed him through the doorway into the front office. Then he turned around. "I don't know who did this, but at this point it's clear Wyatt had something to do with it. At the moment, the money is returned, which is more important than who took it. I think most of us are just thankful that it's back. Everyone, clear out of the hallway so we can gather up the cash and put it back where it belongs. But mark my words: this isn't over. We'll find out who did it eventually, so it would be best if the guilty party stepped forward at a later time. In *private*," the coach added. Then he slammed the office door shut.

"Wow," said Zoe as she looked at my face. "You got your butt *kicked*!"

"Yeah," I said. "Seems like I might be good at that, huh? Maybe I can start a club or something."

Emily pulled a tissue from one of her other purses. Maybe it was her "lunchtime" purse or something. "I think it's manly," she said as she started dabbing my bloody lip with the tissue. Her eyes were cute.

"Gross," said Brayden, cringing.

I laughed but had to hold my side from the pain.

"Chase," said a student from behind. It was one of the members of the ninja clan. "That was the most awesome thing any of us had ever seen in our entire lives. It takes a boy to start a fight, but it takes a man to end one. You ended it with so much honor that my face wants to *melt off!*"

"Cute picture you paint," said Zoe.

The boy continued. "We are without a leader now."

"What about Wyatt?" I asked.

"He's a coward who just wants to control people and show how strong he is," said the boy. "We need a clan leader like you. Brave. Honorable. Able to stand up to bullies. Not beat them down."

I nodded. Ninjas were cool, but this whole thing turned out to be more of a pain than it might've been worth. I smiled with blood on my teeth. "I'll think about it. How's that sound?"

"We'll need to know soon. There are rumors of a pirate invasion in the near future." The boy bowed, as did the rest of the clan, then turned and walked away.

A *pirate* invasion? What kind of insane school *was* this?

"Looks like you might have some friends after all?" Zoe said, laughing.

"Maybe," I said. "That's if I don't get expelled."

"Nobody knows who took the money, and I doubt the teachers here will make any fuss about it," said Brayden. "As long as it's back, they're happy."

Mr. Cooper opened the door to the office and leaned his head out. He pointed at me and said, "Chase, come in here for a moment please."

"Am I in trouble?" I asked as I wiped my lip clean with Emily's tissue.

Mr. Cooper shook his head. "No, it's just that you're a bloody mess. The nurse should have a look at you to make sure you're all right."

I glanced at Zoe and my friends. I didn't want to be lured into the office just to be told I wasn't welcome at the school anymore, but I understood that it might be happening.

"Look, Wyatt already admitted to the whole thing being his fault. He broke down the second I shut this door," Mr. Cooper said. "It really *is* because you're bleeding all over the carpet. What if a parent walked in at this second and saw your battered face?"

"I could probably win a dinosaur-sized lawsuit," I replied.

Zoe laughed. Brayden didn't. Maybe he didn't get it.

Mr. Cooper knocked on the wood of the door. "Just get in here."

I walked to the office door and pushed it open. I could see the top of Wyatt's head over the front counter. He was sitting in the principal's office, probably waiting for his parents. How funny. A ninja getting scolded by his parents.

I turned around and took one last look at Zoe. She nodded at me once, and I returned the gesture. Pushing the door fully open, I stepped into the front office and let it shut behind me.

Buchanan School was a strange place, and though it was new and scary, I'm not sure I'd have it any other way. Besides, I think there's a ninja clan that needs a leader.

My name is Chase Cooper, and I'm a ninja.

diary of a 6th grade ninja 2

pirate invasion

BY MARCUS EMERSON

AND NOAH CHILD

ILLUSTRATED BY DAVID LEE

For my wife,

who hates it when I talk like a pirate . . .

My name is Chase Cooper and since this is my second diary (my dad *still* insists I call it a chronicle), I'll fill you in on what's happened in the last month. But first, a little bit about myself.

Here's my self-portrait. Ladies, please remain calm.

I'm still eleven years old and still a scrawny dude. As much as I want to say being a ninja bulked me up a bunch, it hasn't, but that's a good thing since a beefy ninja would be weird looking.

Buchanan School has been good to me. I was the new kid at the start of the year, but nobody really gave me gruff about it. Cool kids and sports stars fill the hallways between classes, and I do my best to stay off everyone's radar.

I'm what some people might call a comic book nerd, but I prefer the term *aficionado*, which means I'm more of an expert in comics and less of a nerd. It's a term I learned from my cousin, Zoe. She's the coolest cousin in the world, but don't tell her I said that.

I've become better friends with Brayden, the werewolf hunter, but I wouldn't say we're best friends. We've hung out a couple times outside of school to watch bad horror movies and make fun of them. Trust me when I say it's a lot more fun than it sounds. Zoe came over once and even *she* laughed a couple times.

About a month has passed since I finished my first diary chronicle. If you remember, Wyatt was busted for stealing the money raised for the food drive. Since he confessed, there wasn't any reason for the teachers to do any more investigating, so the secret ninja clan is safe and still a secret. You'll also be happy to hear that Wyatt was expelled from Buchanan. I don't know exactly which school he's at right now, and frankly, I don't give a spew about it.

Oh, and all that has led me up to this point, but you've probably figured it out by now. I'm still a ninja, but I'm also the new leader of the ninja clan.

ME →
AGAIN.

DOUBLE
HANDSOME.

I fought it at first for a couple of reasons. One, it was *because* of the ninja clan that I got my butt handed to me during the first week of school. And two, I was only a ninja for less than a week, so how was I supposed to lead an entire clan without any ninjutsu experience? In the end, Zoe convinced me that I shouldn't let the opportunity go, and I finally agreed with her.

Brayden had begged me to let him into the clan, but since I was a new leader, I didn't want it to seem like I was in it just so my friends could join. I told him no, and that he'd have to wait a few months. He wasn't too happy with the decision.

I also agreed to become the leader because the day Wyatt was busted, one of the ninjas approached me and said Buchanan School was in danger of a pirate invasion.

I know, right? Pirates invading a school? I thought it was just a joke . . . As it turns out, it wasn't.

The whole thing can be traced back to early Monday morning in homeroom. How can I remember exactly when it started? Because it was the most annoying thing in the world. It was "Talk Like A Pirate Morning."

"Arrrrrr, mateys!" Brayden said as he entered the room.

I remember sighing the moment I heard him. "Please," I said as I shut my eyes. "Not you too."

"Lighten up," Zoe said, turning around in her seat to face me. "Just 'cause you hate pirates doesn't mean you have to ruin it for the rest of us. Besides, it's just for the morning. It'll stop after homeroom."

"It's not that I hate pirates," I said. "It's that I hate people *talking* like them. But y'know what? It's more that people are *acting* in the middle of school, and not even good acting! They're all just going around yelling, 'Arrrr, matey!'"

"Acting?" Brayden asked. "You mean like in drama club or something?"

"Yeah," I said. "It's *super* annoying."

Zoe curled her lip. "How 'bout you keep it to yourself, then?" She lowered her voice and whispered. "It's not like anyone is making fun of you for dressing in black pajamas during gym class and running around as a ninja."

I shook my head. "Not the same thing."

"I'm sure it's not," Zoe said, nodding her head and giving me a thumbs-up. It was obvious she was mocking me, but she meant it playfully. "*Mister ninja leader.*"

I folded my arms. I hated when she called me that, and she knew it. Being the leader of a ninja clan wasn't easy, and for the past month, I hadn't been sure if I was doing a good job of it. So whenever she called me that, I knew the *name* was a joke, but part of me couldn't help but feel like *I* was actually the joke.

Anyways, everywhere I turned, kids were talking like pirates. It was awful, but I couldn't get away from it, so maybe Zoe was right, and I should lighten up.

"Sorry," I said to Brayden.

"Cool," he replied. "For a second, I thought you were gonna use your awesome nunchuck skills to helicopter out of here. Isn't that what you do? Don't ninjas do that?"

"No," I started to say, but Zoe interrupted me.

"I heard that ninjas can throw an uppercut so fast that it actually travels *backward* in time and punches the *baby* version of the victim!"

"Har har," I said, faking a laugh. "Very funny."

Brayden continued. "I heard that some ninjas just paint themselves black and run around naked because wearing clothes *isn't* hardcore enough. Any truth to that?"

I sighed and sunk down in my seat.

Brayden laughed. "Shiver me timbers! It's only a *joke*, matey!"

My teeth were grinding in my mouth, but I forced a smile. Homeroom was only fifteen minutes long, and all I had to do was wait it out.

The clock on the wall ticked to 7:45 a.m. and the bell rang out, signaling the start of the school day. The homeroom teacher, Mrs. Robinson, leaned back in her chair and started making the announcements for the day.

"*Arrr, mateys!*" said Mrs. Robinson as she cracked a smile and squeezed one eye shut. "Ya scurvy sailors can call me 'One-Eyed Robinson!'"

The entire room full of students shouted, "*Arrrrrr!*"

It would've made me angry if it weren't actually funny. I LOL'd, but so did the rest of the students.

"Here be the announcements, ya scallywags!" Mrs. Robinson continued. She was younger than most teachers and by far the prettiest one at the school. And by *pretty*, I mean she wasn't so old that her face looked like it was trying to run away from her skull. "*Firstly*, I must thank the lot of ya for joinin' me in this wonderful celebration of talkin' like a pirate!"

Several students grumbled in response. I think they were saying, "You're welcome," in their own pirate way. I don't think grammar was too important to them.

"*Secondably*," Mrs. Robinson said, confirming the bit about grammar I just mentioned, "At the end of the week, thar be the event, Dance Till Ya Drop, in which all ye students be required to participate."

It seems Buchanan School hosts an event every month. Last month, it was the food drive. This month, it's an event to raise awareness of cardiovascular diseases and also to help students live healthier lives. The point of Dance Till Ya Drop is to get adults to pledge a certain amount of money for the amount of time you promised to dance for. The whole thing was going to be two hours long, so the idea was to dance the entire two hours anyhow, or at least until you dropped.

"The school will host an assembly at the end of the day on Friday," said Mrs. Robinson. "Then the *official* event be held at five o'clock *sharrrrrp*. The nighttime event be mandatory. Lest ye have an excuse from yer parents, I expect t'see ya thar!"

"Are you going?" I asked Zoe.

She turned in her desk. "Aye, matey. Aren't you?"

I sighed. "If there were any way I could get out of it, I would."

"It'll be fun," said Zoe.

Mrs. Robinson continued talking. "Remember, there be a prize awarded to the student who brings in the most money—a trip fer yer family to Hawaii, and the opportunity to change the Buchanan School mascot!"

That's right. A trip to Hawaii *and* permission to switch the mascot from a wildcat to whatever the winner wanted. Buchanan has had the same mascot for a billion years, and the school was planning on changing it anyway, so I guess they figured making it a prize would get kids to try harder to raise money. They were right.

Mrs. Robinson droned on with a bunch of other announcements nobody really cared about—pizza for lunch, something about graffiti in the boy's bathroom, and stuff about issuing library cards.

Zoe shook her head. She turned around and started whispering. "Seems like a mistake to put the fate of our mascot in the hands of a sixth grader."

"I don't know," Brayden said. "I think it's really cool of them. If I win it, I'm gonna make it an alien. Could you imagine that? The Buchanan Aliens?"

"Yep. Mistake," Zoe said. "*Matey.*"

I rolled my eyes.

Zoe must've noticed because she chuckled at me. "Don't look so stressed. This whole thing might be annoying, but it's all in good fun."

"Sure," I said. "My own cousin has betrayed me . . . speaking like a *pirate* when she *knows* I hate it."

Jabbing me in the shoulder, she spoke again, softer this time. "You know I've got your back no matter what. Even if it means going deep undercover someday, I'll always side with you."

I nodded, glancing at the clock, hoping it was time to dismiss so we could be done with the pirate shenanigans. Thank the stars, because it *was* time to dismiss.

Mrs. Robinson shuffled a few sheets of paper, making sure she had all the announcements, um . . . *announced.* Finally, she smiled and looked up from her notes. "Avast! It be time t'part ways!"

With one last "*Arrrrr,*" everyone started filtering through the door and into the hallway. My next period was art class, which I shared with Zoe and Brayden. Buchanan allowed the sixth graders to set their school schedules to be similar to middle school. They said it made the transition into seventh grade smoother and less traumatic, but I had my doubts about that.

Monday. 8:15 a.m. Art class.

When I arrived at art class, Zoe and Brayden were already there and talking to a new student. The kid was sitting at the desk next to Zoe's, which happened to be my desk, but since I'm such a cool guy, I didn't say anything.

"Just so you know," I said. "That's my seat."

Okay, maybe I said a *little* something.

"Sorry, mate," said the new kid as he lifted his book bag off the floor. "But don't ye know that nothing's sacred in a pirate *invasion*?"

I put my hand out, gesturing for him to stop speaking. It looked like I was telling him I knew what he was saying, but really, I was only trying to get him to shut his pirate mouth. The art desks were arranged in clumps of four, and the two directly across from him were empty so I took a seat in one of those. The sixth graders didn't have assigned seats anyways, so it's not like I could've done anything. "Nobody sits over here. You can have that desk."

The new kid smiled. "Thank ye, kind sir."

I raised my eyebrows. "But only if you stop talking like a pirate."

Just then, Mr. Richardson entered the room and let out a shout. "Arrrr, mateys!"

Great, I thought. Apparently, the art teacher didn't get the memo about how talking like a pirate was supposed to be *only* during homeroom. The entire class erupted in laughter and replied to him in the same way.

"Seems we have a new student joinin' us today," Mr. Richardson said. "Everybody welcome Carlyle."

Zoe turned to face the new kid. "Cool name."

"I have my parents to thank for that," Carlyle said.

CARLYLE.

This made Zoe giggle in a weird way. I also noticed that her eyelashes fluttered. Gross. My cousin just fell in crush at first sight.

I didn't want to be rude to Carlyle since I was pretty new at the school myself, but honestly, I was happy I wasn't the *newest* kid anymore. I leaned forward in my desk. "It's nice to meet you, Carlyle. My name's Chase."

The new kid stared at me for a moment. The awkward silence was definitely *awkward*. Finally, his lips cracked a smirk. "Ahoy, Chase. Pleasure to make yer acquaintance."

I tightened a smile and ignored the way he spoke. Luckily it was Brayden that said something.

"Oh, that whole pirate thing was just for homeroom," said Brayden.

Zoe jumped to Carlyle's defense. "So what if he wants to keep it going? I think it's pretty cool if he did. Besides, Richardson spoke like that when he walked into the room. Maybe it should be the entire *day*."

Brayden raised his hands in surrender. "You're right. Nothing wrong with that."

Carlyle slowly turned toward me and spoke. "Do ya mind, matey? If I were to speak to ya in pirate tongue?"

It took all my strength to look at him and not laugh. "Not at all. It's a free country."

Monday. 10:30 a.m. Gym class.

To be honest, the rest of art class wasn't horrible. For being the new kid, Carlyle seemed like a stand-up guy. He hit it off instantly with most of the others in class with the way he continued to speak like a pirate. Part of me was impressed that a new kid at a new school would have the guts to do something so odd on his first day. He even made a few jokes that made me laugh.

So all that to say I didn't mind seeing him in the same gym class as Zoe, Brayden, and I. Obviously Zoe was a little more excited than I was.

Brayden and I had already changed into our gym clothes and were waiting out on the basketball court for the other students and the gym teacher, Mr. Cooper, to arrive.

When Carlyle walked out of the locker room, he joined us, probably since we just had art class together and we were the only kids he knew.

"OMG!" cried Zoe as she exited the girls' locker room. "I can't believe you're in *this* class too!"

Carlyle nodded. "Aye."

ZOE

"Well, that's just . . . " Zoe said with a twinkle in her eye. "That's just *somethin'*, ain't it?"

When the rest of the students were standing on the gymnasium floor, Mr. Cooper started making the rounds, checking off names from the attendance list. After he checked my name off, he looked at Carlyle.

"New kid, huh?" Mr. Cooper said without looking up from his clipboard. "Carlyle's your name?"

"And plunderin's me game," Carlyle said.

Mr. Cooper's face didn't move. "Nice," he said with no emotion, scratching a checkmark on his clipboard. Then he looked up and spoke loudly. "Same as before, children. Basketball in here, soccer out on the field, or laps around the track for the unmotivated. For anyone interested, there's some sort of obstacle course out there, or whatever . . . I don't care. Do what you feel like."

It was pretty obvious Mr. Cooper didn't love his job.

I started walking swiftly to the gym doors but slowed down once I realized Brayden and Zoe weren't keeping up. They were lagging behind, talking to Carlyle.

"So where did you move here from?" Zoe asked.

Carlyle scratched the back of his head. "Oh no, my family didn't move or anything. I open enrolled so I could attend here. I heard some pretty nice things about you guys."

"Like what?" I asked, happy that Carlyle had stopped the pirate nonsense.

"Like the way Buchanan allows sixth graders more freedom than other schools."

"What school did you come from?" Brayden asked.

"Williams," Carlyle replied.

Brayden gasped quietly. "That's where Wyatt was shipped off to."

So that's where he was forced to go, I thought. "I guess it's lucky Carlyle got out of there while he could then," I said.

Carlyle paused. "Who's Wyatt?"

Zoe shrugged her shoulders. "No one special. Just a bully who used to go here, but he was expelled after the first week of school."

"Really?" Carlyle said. "For what?"

Zoe started fumbling over some words about theft and a fight. I could tell she wasn't comfortable exposing me as the kid who got beat up, so I saved her the trouble of doing so.

"He beat me up," I said calmly. "Pretty bad, too."

Carlyle's eyebrows rose. "Wow."

Zoe came to my defense. "No, it's not that he just beat you up. You stood your ground and *refused* to hit him back. So sure, he mopped the floor with your butt, but you basically *allowed* him to."

"Ah," said Carlyle with a smile. "The hero of Buchanan then. That's what you are."

Hero wasn't exactly a term I was comfortable with. "My cousin exaggerates."

"She's your cousin?" Carlyle asked, surprised.

"Yeah," Zoe said. "And proud of it."

I would've felt embarrassed if I hadn't suddenly stepped into the shadow of the obstacle course Mr. Cooper had hinted about. Zoe, Brayden, and Carlyle stopped in their tracks behind me, gasping as they looked up.

The obstacle course was enormous. It spanned almost the entire field in the center of the track. In my head, I imagined that it was probably some kind of adult bounce house, but this definitely *wasn't* that.

"Holy moly," Brayden whispered.

I just nodded in silence.

The start of the course was a rope bridge that sprawled over a huge pool of water. Right after the bridge was a rock wall that didn't have any floor beneath it. The kid running the course would have to grab one of the handholds of the wall while swinging from the rope bridge. At the top of the wall was a zip line with handlebars you had to grab.

After that point, it was difficult to see the rest of the course. There were walls among walls blocking the view. It looked like there were spinning pillars scattered throughout it. I saw other pools of water and mud that the runner would have to avoid or worse yet, swim across. At the end of the course, there was a flat open space with barriers scattered throughout. High above the open space was a gun that shot tennis balls the runner had to avoid.

The course was a *monster.*

"Beauty, ain't she?" Mr. Cooper said proudly as he approached us. "Just got her imported from *Norway.* The pamphlet said it was something that the Vikings themselves trained with, but somehow I doubt that. It also says ninety nine percent of students who attempt it can't make it past the first rope bridge."

"What's it doing here?" Carlyle asked. "Will students be running it today?"

Mr. Cooper shook his head. "Oh no, it's not ready by any means. Legally, I mean, buuuuut . . ." the gym teacher trailed off as he glanced over his shoulder. "If I don't see nothin'."

"Race ya," Brayden said, smiling at me.

"How can I possibly say no?" I asked as I started running toward the obstacle course at full speed.

When I reached the rope bridge, I didn't hesitate and started climbing. Grabbing the ropes, I balanced myself and walked as quickly as possible over the pool of water. I wasn't sure how deep it was, but I didn't feel like finding out firsthand.

Carefully, I stepped each foot over the other on the thick rope. I wanted to look back and see how far behind Brayden was, but this part of the bridge demanded my full attention. It really didn't matter how far behind he was as long as he was *behind.*

Once I reached the end of the rope, I had to jump across and catch the rock wall that looked a mile away. I took the opportunity to catch my breath and make fun of Brayden, but when I turned around, he wasn't there.

I had to spin in a full circle to see that Brayden was still talking to Carlyle and Zoe outside the obstacle course. That dumb-hole didn't even follow me onto the course!

"Hey!" I shouted. "I'm *winning!*"

Brayden looked over at me, apparently too busy talking with the new kid to realize he was losing the race. Whatever Carlyle was saying to him must've been important, because Brayden had folded his arms and was nodding in some sort of understanding. Then I saw the two of them shake hands before Carlyle started walking back toward the school.

Whatever, I thought as I turned around. I was about to dominate this Norwegian obstacle course. I didn't need Brayden tagging along.

With all my strength, I jumped from the rope and reached for the rock wall. I could feel the handhold in my fingers as I stretched my body out. All I had to do was firmly grab it . . .

But I didn't.

I fell face first into the pool of water underneath me. All I can remember thinking was, "I'm glad this water was here to break my fall."

When I came up for air, Zoe and Brayden were laughing at me. It was embarrassing.

After I jumped out of the pool, I told them to walk the track without me since I had to dry off, but the truth was that I had a meeting with my ninja clan I had to attend. My wet clothing would have to wait.

About five minutes later, I found my way to the secret passage through the border of the woods at the edge of the school's track. Before I came along, the clan had salvaged some old lockers the school had tried to throw away. Now they were used to store all the ninja outfits, so they didn't have to wear them under their clothing all day long. I heard they tried that when they first started, but the stench from the outfits was just too foul after about a week.

After slipping into my ninja outfit, I stepped out from the lockers. The entire ninja clan straightened their posture at the sight of me. They punched their open palms and bowed out of respect. I'd been their leader for an entire month, and it still felt weird when they did that.

"That's enough," I said through my black mask as I patted the air in front of me.

"What's on the agenda for today, sir?" one of the ninjas asked me.

"Nothing in particular," I said. "The usual, I guess. Everything seems to be going okay?"

Several of the ninjas nodded at me. A few of them sighed.

I put my arms out and shrugged my shoulders. "Buchanan seems to be doing fine! I mean, if there were any kind of suspicious activity going on, it might be different, but . . . what did you guys do *before* I was the leader?"

The ninja in front of me answered. "The first week of school was spent sneaking around corridors and stealing all that money and stuff."

"Right," I said. "Which is something we're *not* going to do. What about last year? What'd you guys do?"

"Snuck around corridors mostly," said the ninja. "Stole some things from here and there."

Standing in front of the ninja clan was awful. They all understood Wyatt was a bully and that it had been necessary to remove him from leadership, but I felt like I was also failing them as their new leader. I know they were bored, but I couldn't give the order to *steal* stuff! "Ninjas don't just steal things, you know."

I heard many of the kids sigh, disappointed. A few of them returned to their slouching position while others folded their arms or placed their hands on their hips. The first week I was their leader, they never would've presented themselves in such a way. I hated to even think it, but I could feel their respect for me washing away.

"So we continue to train out here?" the ninja in front of me asked. "Like *every single day* for the past *month*?"

I shook my head. "Yeah. I guess for now, until I can think of something better to do, we'll just continue our training. You guys can make those paper ninja stars, too, if you want."

"There's no point in practicing ninjutsu if we're never gonna use it," said one of the girl ninjas in the back. "I just wish we knew what we were training for."

Under my mask, I whispered, "Me too . . . me too."

Tuesday. 7:45 a.m. Homeroom.

As always, I was the last in the room before the bell rang. Even though there weren't assigned seats, all the students tried to sit in the same spot every day. The seat behind Zoe was unofficially mine. I dropped my bag on the desk and sat.

"You know you're almost late every day?" Zoe asked.

"Yeah," I said. "Maybe I'll fix that someday."

"Careful, mate," said one of the students next to me, "Or it be Davy Jones's locker for ya!"

I rolled my eyes. "You know that ended almost twenty-four hours ago, right?"

The boy smiled. "There be a black spot on ya, matey."

I glanced down at my shirt, but didn't see what he was talking about.

The boy leaned back in his chair. "Yer days be numbered, is alls I'm sayin'."

"Sure," I said, annoyed by the way he was chewing his lips. I thought it best to ignore him, so I turned back to Zoe and tapped on her shoulder. "Hey, can I ask you something?"

Zoe spun in her desk, excited that I needed her advice. She set her hand on mine and spoke tenderly. "Of course. You can ask me *anything*."

I laughed, pulling my hand away from hers. "Weirdo!"

Zoe laughed too. "I know. It took *all* my strength to keep a straight face just now."

I wiped the tear from my eye. "But seriously, I think I need help."

"Oh," she said, surprised. "Um, okay. Does this have to do with talking to girls? Because it's actually *much* easier than you're making it. I know you think keeping your eyes closed as you talk makes you look laid back, but it actually just makes you look creepy."

"No!" I said. "It's about my *ninja clan*."

"Ohhhhh," Zoe sighed. "Nerd stuff. I'm still not interested in joining, if that's what you're going to ask."

"No, nothing like that. I think that maybe I'm not cut out to be their leader . . . "

Zoe's brow furrowed. "Go on."

"Those kids are bored with me, and I'm not sure how to liven them up. All we've been doing is training every day."

"Nothing wrong with that."

"No, you're right, but I can tell they all want a little more excitement. And I don't know how to give it to them."

"What'd they do before you were the leader?" Zoe asked.

"Stole stuff and tried framing it on you," I replied.

"Ohhhh, riiiiiight. Yeah, I think it'd be smart if you *didn't* do that kind of stuff again."

"Me too," I said. "I spent most of last night studying up on leadership and stuff. It suggested I start with communicating the problem with the group and then hearing them out. Like, ask their opinions and ideas."

"Maybe it's just *me* . . . ," Zoe began, one eyebrow raised high, "but a ninja clan that ran like it was some kind of club or something? I think that'd be the lamest, most boring ninja clan in the entire *history* of ninja clans."

"That's saying something, coming from you."

"I *know.* I love resolving issues and clubs and stuff!"

Zoe made a good point, but it didn't help me feel any better. The ninjas were getting bored, and I was determined to figure out a way they could be useful, even if it meant having lame board meetings and brainstorming sessions. Nothing I was doing felt like it was working anyways, so what could it hurt?

"What do ninjas do?" Zoe asked. "Don't they just sit around, hiding for hours in dark shadows until the target comes around? And then, don't they just go nuts in a blaze of black smoke and burn villages down?"

"Um," I grunted. "We're gonna do this again?"

I turned around and looked at Brayden, expecting a barrage of ninja jokes and insults hurled toward me, but they never came. Instead, he tapped at his desk nervously and tried to smile. His eye even twitched.

Have you ever seen a sixth grader fake a smile? It's a sure sign that something is off.

"What's up?" I asked. "Your eye just did a thing."

He rubbed his eyes with his hands. "Yeah, I'm just tired. That's all. I got to bed late last night."

"Oh yeah?" Zoe asked. "Studying up on werewolves and stuff?"

Glancing at the clock, Brayden nodded. "Sure. That's it. Werewolf stuff."

Brayden was acting so strangely that it was just uncomfortable. I decided to leave it at that, though. If he acted weird in gym, maybe I'd say something again.

I hoped he didn't.

Tuesday. 10:45 a.m. Gym class.

Brayden had acted a little strange for the remainder of homeroom, but by the time art class started, he seemed to be back to normal. When Carlyle started talking to him, he completely chilled out.

Oh, and Carlyle was *still* talking like a pirate. I made sure to look angry and say a couple of quick snips here and there, y'know, all sarcastic like. I'm pretty sure he could tell I wasn't happy about it. Zoe and Brayden were eating it up, though.

In fact, by the time we were out on the track, they didn't even notice that I wasn't walking with them. Carlyle was telling funny stories of his old school in his charming pirate language, and Zoe and Brayden were almost hypnotized by it. Seriously, did this kid think he was gonna go the whole school year doing this? What happens when he gets to middle school? High school? College?

The bottom line? It was *eerie*. Carlyle was *eerie*. I just hoped Zoe and Brayden would see it eventually.

When I knew I was alone, I slipped into the wooded area by the track. The ninja clan was waiting, and after all my research the night before, I was actually looking forward to hearing some suggestions from the other ninjas. For the first time in the past month, I felt like things were going to turn around.

Unfortunately, I was in for a big surprise when I showed up for the meeting. After I geared up in my ninja outfit, I walked out, expecting to see the ninjas waiting for me, but that's not exactly what happened. When I stepped out, I saw that half of my ninja clan was absent.

The half that *did* show up punched their palms and bowed to me. I bowed back.

"What gives?" I asked. "Was there some kind of assembly or something today?"

The ninjas grumbled and looked nervously at one another, but nobody answered me.

"Come on," I said. "Is there something else going on today that I don't know about?"

A shorter member stepped forward and stared at the ground. "Sir," he said softly. "The others . . . they've decided it was time for them to . . . "

He was so quiet it was driving me crazy. "What? *Speak up!* Where's everyone at?"

The ninja looked into my eyes and spoke boldly. "They've decided it was time for them to walk away from this, sir. It was time for them to hang up their ninja robes and move onto greener pastures."

"Greener pastures?"

"It means 'better things.'"

"I *know* what it means," I said, upset. "It's . . . I guess . . . I'm a little *shocked,* is all."

"Shouldn't be," said one of the ninjas from the back. "This group is getting lame. What else did he think was gonna happen?"

I wanted to shout at that ninja, but I felt like I had been punched in the gut. Half of my ninja clan had quit, and all I could do was blame myself. When I looked up, I noticed that the other ninjas were awaiting my orders, but I didn't have any. I looked at each of the remaining members before I noticed that one of the ninjas in the back wasn't wearing his proper ninja robes.

When I squinted, I saw that the ninja was only wearing a black sheet draped over him. "You there," I said. "What's with the cape?"

At that moment, the kid flipped the cape off and jumped through the trees. It wasn't someone I recognized and right before he disappeared, I swear it looked like he was wearing . . . an *eye patch?*

I didn't waste any time and started sprinting through the wooded area of the ninja hideout. From behind I could hear the other ninjas start following me, but because they were all action junkies, I knew this kid would be dead meat if they caught him.

"No!" I shouted at them. "I'll handle this! Everyone stay here and keep training!"

SPY!

When I burst from the trees, I could see that the kid was running as fast as he could through the grass and toward the school. He had already passed the Norwegian obstacle course. His black cape was flapping wildly behind him as his fat boots stomped on the ground. It was clear as day. This kid was dressed like a pirate, which I would've made fun of, but then I remembered I was dressed as a ninja.

I started running through the field, ignoring all the kids who were probably pointing and laughing at me. From the corner of my eye, I saw Zoe and Brayden walking along the track, but Carlyle wasn't with them.

As soon as the costumed spy reached the school building, he entered through one of the doors next to the cafeteria. I did my best to keep up with him, but it still took me about thirty seconds to make it to the door.

The cafeteria windows were only a few feet away, and I could see that one of the lunches had already started. If I entered through this door in a ninja outfit and someone saw me . . . it wouldn't be the *worst* thing to happen to me, but it definitely wouldn't be good for my social life. My street clothes were still sitting in the woods, too far to retrieve now. If I waited much longer, I risked losing the spy.

I decided to man up and go inside.

Inside, the room was dark, but far from quiet. I let the door shut behind me as I found a nice shadowy area to hide in. I was on the stage that was attached to the cafeteria. A heavy curtain blocked the students from seeing anything on the stage at the moment. I smiled to myself, happy that the darkness was my friend.

The spy was nowhere to be seen, at least not right away. I could see shadows from the cafeteria moving under the curtain, but I could also see some movement coming from the center of the stage up ahead.

Looking to my left, I saw a thin metal ladder that reached into a dark area above me. Once my eyes adjusted, I could see a catwalk spanning the entire stage area. With my black ninja robes and the low light, I'd be nearly impossible to see up there.

When I reached the top of the ladder, I crouched down and walked as quietly as possible over the spot where I'd seen movement. From up here, I could see everything on the stage. There must've been almost forty kids moving around and working on various things. The noise from the cafeteria was enough that these guys didn't worry about anyone hearing them.

A few of the kids were working on different things in separate corners of the stage. It looked oddly familiar, as if they were training for something. Most of the other kids were gathered near the center of the stage so I crawled out farther to get a glimpse of what they were looking at. The spy that was in my meeting was among them.

The kids were huddled closely and looking at something on the ground, but that wasn't the strangest part. In all the excitement, I guess I didn't realize until that moment that *all* the kids were dressed in pirate uniforms and talking in that annoying pirate tongue! Gross, right? But I also noticed that they each wore some kind of necklace that had a skull embedded into the little pendant on it. Pirates must've gotten them when they joined the club. I wondered if maybe my ninja clan would appreciate something like that.

Then, to my surprise, the group backed away from their spot. Carlyle was at the center of the huddle, looking down at a large piece of cloth laid out before him. He started nodding and patting the other pirates' shoulders. When Carlyle was far enough away from the cloth, I was able to see it better.

It was a blue rectangle that had the words "Buchanan Buccaneers" sewn into it with yellow fabric. At the center of the rectangle was a drawing of a pirate ship.

"They're making a flag?" I whispered.

The instant I whispered, all of the pirates jumped back and stood on guard. Of course, it would be my luck that a whisper would tip them off to the fact that I was up here, but I let out a sigh of relief when I saw that it wasn't *me* that spooked them.

A sliver of light crawled across the floor as the curtain was pushed aside. Mr. Cooper leaned through the opening. "Excuse me! What're you kids doing in here?"

Carlyle gestured for the other pirates to stand down as he stepped forward. "Mr. Cooper. My apologies, but we're in the middle of rehearsing a play for the school. Why else would we be on this stage dressed in pirate costumes?"

"You're supposed to be out on the track, young man," Mr. Cooper said. "You're in my gym class right now, so tell me how you've somehow found your way in *here?*"

"I thought someone told you?" Carlyle said, flabbergasted. "I mean, they said they were going to tell you that I was needed in here for the next week or so."

"I hadn't heard anything," said Mr. Cooper. "Don't you worry, son. I'll get to the bottom of this."

"Wait," said Carlyle. "How would you like a small part in the play?"

Mr. Cooper tightened his lips.

"There's an open spot for a blundering idiot," said Carlyle bravely. "All you'd have to do is hang out on stage during a certain scene and yell out some hilarious insults!"

Mr. Cooper stared at Carlyle. I could tell from the look in his eye that Carlyle was *busted.* "So I'd actually have a speaking role?"

What? Was Mr. Cooper actually considering it?

"Absolutely," said Carlyle. "I'll have your script for you tomorrow, sir."

Mr. Cooper nodded, but only once. "Tomorrow."

I couldn't believe what I was seeing! Carlyle had built a gang of pirates who were doing something that was at least *questionable*, and Mr. Cooper had just given them a nod of approval! This was insane!

I was going to have to confront Carlyle on my own, but I would need help from my ninja clan. When I climbed down from the ladder, I snuck over to the side door I had snuck through.

"Hey," said a voice from out of nowhere.

My heart dropped as I turned around. There was a bright flash of light in my eyes. As I reached my hands up, I heard the door click open behind me, and then I felt someone push against my chest until I was outside the school and on my butt in the gravel.

Wednesday. 7:45 a.m. Homeroom.

Nice cliffhanger back there, huh? I thought it was more exciting to end the diary entry at that spot because the stuff that happened afterward was boring. All I did was dust myself off, change back into my street clothes, and spend the rest of the day wondering who it was that pushed me out the door. I didn't get a look at the kid—the door slammed shut and locked before I knew what happened. My face got a little scratched up, but that's about it.

"What's up with your face?" Zoe asked when I took the seat behind her.

I touched the scratches on my cheek. "Nothing. I biffed on my skateboard last night."

"And caught yourself with your face?"

I nodded.

Mrs. Robinson rose from her desk as soon as the bell rang. "Ahoy, children."

Come on! It was *Wednesday!* Two days after that ridiculous pirate morning! There were a couple of small laughs among the students.

The teacher shrugged her shoulders and continued with the announcements. "As you know, Dance Till Ya Drop is scheduled for five p.m. this Friday night. If you're not staying after school to help on Friday, then have your parents drop you off around four thirty. You'll need some time to sign in. The winner of the event will hopefully be announced that night, so be sure to bring all the money you've raised. Once you've turned it in at the front table, you'll proceed to the cafeteria and wait for the event to kick off. While students are dancing, a few select teachers will be given the task of counting the money, so we should know the winner by the time the event is finished."

Zoe turned around. "How much have you raised?"

"Not a lot," I said.

"Did you even try?"

"Not really," I replied. "I went to a couple houses on my street, but nobody opened their door to me. A couple people even turned their lights off and yelled that they weren't home after I rang their doorbell."

Zoe chuckled. "I don't think I raised enough to win, but I got a pretty good chunk, I think. My dad took it to his work and got his friends to donate."

Remember that her dad was my uncle—brother to *my* dad. "You think Uncle John would do that for me too?"

Zoe's jaw dropped, apparently shocked that I would suggest that. "It was a *joke*," I said.

"Better be," Zoe said as she started turning back toward the front of the class but stopped as something caught her eye. She pointed to my book bag. "What's that under your backpack?"

I looked down. There was a rolled-up sheet of paper sticking out from beneath my seat. The last time I received an anonymous letter like this, it was when the ninja clan wanted to recruit me. Hopefully, this was just from a girl or something.

"Maybe someone wants to give you cookies and soda again," Zoe said with a smirk.

I reached under the bag and pulled the paper out. "Weird," I said. "This paper is really old and crusty, and look at this . . . there's a wax seal holding it shut."

Zoe's eyes widened. "Pirates . . . "

I peeled away the wax seal and opened the sheet of parchment. *Please be from a girl,* I hoped. It definitely wasn't.

Salutations Chase,

Be in the boys' locker room during gym class today or suffer the consequences.

The Captain.

"Why are all your notes from boys?" Zoe joked.

I took a breath. "I can't *wait* until I actually get a real note from a girl."

Wednesday. 10:40 a.m. Gym class.

It wasn't easy for me to stay in the locker room. All the other students dressed and left the room already. Mr. Cooper was always the last one out precisely *because* of stragglers who tried to hide until class started so they could skip. I figured out a foolproof way of remaining in the room, though.

"Chase?" Mr. Cooper asked. "You okay in there?"

I groaned in the locked bathroom stall. "I'm not feeling so good, coach. I think I caught a bug or something."

"That's fine, son," said the coach. "But you're going to have to see the nurse, then. I can't have you sitting in here on your own."

"I know," I said, sitting on the toilet seat. Just to clarify so it's not gross, I had my pants pulled up. I was faking. "But my stomach feels like it's bubbling or something . . . I'm not sure I can make it there at the moment."

Mr. Cooper sighed from outside the stall.

"Can I just sit here for a minute or two?" I asked with my voice barely above a whisper.

The coach paused before he spoke again. "Sure. Take as long as you need, all right?" he said. "Just don't take *too* long."

"Ten four," I said. "Thanks, coach."

I listened to Mr. Cooper's footsteps echo against the concrete floor of the locker room until I heard the squeaking of the locker room doors open and then slam shut. As soon as I knew he was out of the room, I opened the stall door and started scanning the area.

I was still in my street clothes. I thought that changing into my ninja robes in front of everyone would've been obvious, plus the kid who delivered the note already knew I was a ninja . . . in fact, I don't know why I think it's such a secret. I'm pretty sure *everyone* knows.

I searched each corner of the locker room, but there was nobody else in there. There was a stillness that sent chills down my spine. Every time I peeked around some lockers, my heart stopped, expecting to see pirates, but there was nothing.

And then the locker room doors opened from across the room. I heard the sound of boots clunking on the cold concrete floors as I stood in place, ready to meet with the pirates head on.

Carlyle stepped around the corner and stopped in place, several feet away from me. Two other pirates, both wearing gigantic, dumb-looking pirate hats that covered their faces in shadows, accompanied him.

"Ahoy," said Carlyle. "I see the note was delivered to ya successfully."

I wasn't sure how to respond. "*Duh.*"

Carlyle let out a short laugh. "Seems ya found our secret hideout while you were poking your nose around where it shouldn't have been."

"I only followed the spy you sent to *my* hideout," I said coldly.

"Right," Carlyle said. "But it still doesn't change the fact that you were where ya weren't supposed to be. And that means ya *saw* stuff ya weren't supposed to *see*."

I nodded and narrowed my eyes. "Uh yeah. Again, I only ended up there because *you* sent a spy into my clan."

The pirates behind Carlyle stepped forward aggressively, but their captain lifted his hand, signaling them to remain at ease. "Seems we got ourselves quite a conundrum."

"A what?" I asked.

"A *conundrum*," Carlyle repeated. "Too big a word for ya, matey? It means we've got ourselves a *problem*."

"Seems we do," I said. "I don't know what it is that you're planning, but I know that it can't be good."

"So the question begs . . . *why* ain't you gone to the authorities yet?"

I paused. "I had to build a case. If I went to the teachers and told them a bunch of kids dressed as pirates were running around the school, then they'd probably look at me like I was crazy."

Carlyle bellowed a mighty laugh at that. "Of *course* they would! Especially since you're the kid that runs around in a ninja outfit!" Then his face grew dark and sinister. "This be a fight ya ain't prepared for, mate. Soon I'll have the entire school in the palm of my hands . . . and you'll be but a fleck of dust blowing in the wind."

This time, I was the one who laughed. "What do you think you're going to do? You're just a kid *dressed* as a pirate! You really think you're going to do something destructive at Buchanan? The last kid that tried that was booted to another school district."

"Leave Wyatt out of this!" Carlyle screamed suddenly, spitting everywhere. "You're the reason he's not at this school anymore, and in this life or the next, *we'll* have our revenge!"

My legs felt numb as I took a step back. I clenched my fists, trying to hide the fact that my hands were shaking. This kid was intimidating, that's for sure, and I was afraid of him. "What do you mean . . . *we*?"

Carlyle straightened his posture and wiped the spit off his chin. "You see, you *pathetic ninja*, Wyatt is my *cousin*."

Suddenly, my head felt dizzy. It was like the room had started spinning.

"When he told me of how you got him expelled from this school," Carlyle said. "I felt sorry for him. When he told me of how you stole his entire ninja clan . . . I promised to avenge him."

I leaned against the cold metal lockers behind me in case I passed out. "What are you saying?"

"Are you daft?" Carlyle asked. "I'm saying that I enrolled at this school so I could get closer to *you*. You've already seen that I've built an army of pirates, and it's only getting bigger. Soon, the pirate invasion will be complete, and Buchanan will be *owned* by pirates."

"That's insane," I growled. "And how exactly is a sixth grader going to take over an entire school like that?"

Carlyle smirked. "You saw the flag we were building, did you not?"

"The Buchanan Buccaneers?" I said, and then it finally hit me. I tried to speak loudly, but my lungs felt empty. "That flag is for the new mascot . . . "

"Aye, mate," said Carlyle. "I've made sure my victory is secured for the event on Friday night. My followers at this school have agreed to give *all* their fundraiser money to me so I'd be the one with the most collected. As the winner . . . I'll have complete control over what the new mascot will be. Once it's changed to the Buccaneers, . . . the pirate invasion part of my plan will be complete."

"Pirate invasion part? Is there *another* part?"

"The destruction of you."

I leaned forward and stuck out my chest. "If it's a fight you're looking for—"

Carlyle raised his open palm to me. "Nay. Wyatt's the fighter in the family."

I was confused. "Then . . . what?"

"It's already started," Carlyle said. "I'll destroy your spirit by taking what's important to you."

"The ninja clan," I whispered.

"Aye," he replied. "Yer ninjas . . . yer friends . . . and yer very own cousin."

That was too far. "Leave Zoe out of this!"

One of Carlyle's pirate bodyguards stepped forward. He removed his hat and turned to face me. I was in shock.

"Brayden?" I whispered.

"Seems he's had a problem joinin' your clan for a while," Carlyle laughed. "Well, we pirates don't discriminate like that. All are welcome to join here."

"Sorry, matey," said Brayden.

"If it wasn't for Mister Brayden here, then we wouldn't have known you were sneakin' around above the stage yesterday," said Carlyle.

"You saw me?" I asked my friend.

Carlyle answered for him. "He's the one that pushed ya out the door, but not before snapping a photo of you as proof."

Brayden lowered his gaze. "I didn't know it was you."

Carlyle spoke swiftly. "It still doesn't change the fact that he turned ya in even *after* he saw it was *you* in the photos."

Brayden didn't say anything. My closest friend at Buchanan had betrayed me, and why? Because I wouldn't let him become a ninja? He was wearing the gold pendant with the skull around his neck. The sign of a pirate.

"Brayden," I said.

"Ya got a black mark on ya," said Brayden.

I looked down at my shirt again. Where was this black spot everyone was talking about?

"It means you're marked," Brayden said with a sigh. "That your days are numbered. It's like a giant target."

"Oh," I said as I stared at the floor.

"I'll accept your surrender by Friday," said Carlyle bluntly. "You can deliver it in the form of your silly ninja robe.

"And if I don't?" I asked.

"Then Zoe will have to pay," Brayden said. "They'll make her walk the plank."

"The plank?" I cried out. It was silly to think of such a thing, but then I realized that a pirate invasion was silly too, but here I was in the midst of one. "You'd better—"

The pirate bodyguards stepped in front of Carlyle. This time, the captain allowed it. They forced me against the lockers and held me in place as I watched Carlyle walk toward the exit of the locker room.

"Friday, Chase," said Carlyle without looking back. "I'll expect your ninja robes by Friday, or else it's Zoe who'll pay." He stopped just before the door. "And if ye tell anyone about this meeting, I promise you'll regret it."

The bodyguards let me drop to my feet when their captain was gone. Brayden didn't look at my eyes the entire time, and I didn't say anything to him. When they left the locker room, there was a silence in the air that felt like it was going to crush my skull.

Why was Zoe always the target for the bad guys?

Thursday. 10:45 a.m. Gym class.

It hadn't been easy sitting across from Carlyle in art class, but I did it. It sickened me to watch Zoe flirt with him. I wanted to speak out, but was too afraid of what the pirate captain would do. Brayden sat in the clump of desks behind us. He didn't turn around once. In fact, we hadn't said a word to each other all morning.

But that was this morning, and it was time for gym, which also meant it was time to meet with my ninja clan. I knew the remaining members could help me figure out what to do next. Part of me was even excited that I'd be able to give them some excitement for the first time in a month.

I snuck through the entrance at the side of the woods and jogged to the lockers. As I put my gear on, I tried to think of the best way to expose Carlyle and his band of pirates.

During lunch, we could pull the cords to the stage curtain, letting it fall to the floor. Everyone in the cafeteria would see them playing around in their silly costumes, and hopefully they'd make fun of Carlyle so bad his pirate followers would abandon him.

Or I could go straight to the principal and tell him Carlyle's plan. It would sound insane coming from me, but if I was able to prove he was Wyatt's cousin, I think the principal would at *least* hear me out.

Or the remaining members of my clan and I could confront the pirates and wage an all-out war with them. Starting a huge fight wasn't ideal, but at this point, it wasn't out of the question. Maybe a giant fight like that would reveal all of Carlyle's plans.

But it didn't matter. No plan I could think of was going to be worth anything, because when I stepped through the foliage, I saw that the secret hideout was completely empty. There wasn't a single member of my ninja clan waiting.

"Hello?" I said loudly. The only answer came from the wind sifting through the leaves.

Wonderful, I thought. Absolutely wonderful. Just when I think I can be a good leader, I lose my ninja clan.

If I had been a better leader—no, . . . not a *better* leader. I just needed to be a more *exciting* leader. I just needed to give them a little bit of the adventure they wanted, and now that I *had* it . . . it was too late.

With nothing left to lose, I made the decision to go back to the cafeteria. I wasn't okay with sitting in the hideout by myself and pouting, so maybe I could have another discussion with Carlyle. I had no idea what I was going to say, but hopefully it would come to me in the moment. After I changed out of my ninja uniform, I folded it neatly and held it under my arm. Normally, I would've stuffed it back into my locker, but I wasn't a hundred percent sure I was going to keep it.

Thursday. 11:20 a.m. Gym class.

It says "gym class," but I was obviously running around outside of it. I don't recommend you do the same. You could get in a load of trouble, unless you were trying to stop a huge pirate invasion. I guess in that case, maybe it's all right.

By this time, I had snuck back into the stage area of the cafeteria. I didn't step out right away, but instead, I stood by the door. I wasn't sure what I was waiting for. Maybe there was a part of me that wanted to walk away and fight.

I can't know for sure what I was feeling at that moment, because a pirate stepped out from the stage and froze in his tracks when he saw me. My heart stopped for half a beat as I waited for him to yell for his pirate buddies. But then I saw that it wasn't a *boy* pirate, but a *girl*.

She stepped backward. Her face was completely covered in shadow, so I wasn't sure who it was, and apparently she wasn't keen on letting me find out. She spun around and started running down the side of the stage area.

I didn't know what to do, so I let my instinct take over and started chasing after her.

Whoever it was, she was fast—faster than any girl *I'd* ever raced against, at least, which probably isn't saying much since I'm not exactly what you'd call "athletic."

She jumped over boxes in a single leap, even sliding her body against the wall so her landing was smooth. For a second, I thought about trying it, but I knew my legs would betray me, so I ran around the boxes.

The other pirates were too busy talking and training with swords to notice that a boy was chasing a girl backstage. The noise of the students eating lunch in the cafeteria made sure our footsteps weren't heard.

I wanted to shout, but knew I couldn't unless I wanted a bunch of pirates to chase after me.

She was nearly ten feet away, and her speed was making that gap even longer. My legs were straining from running and dodging obstacles. I knew if I continued, she'd eventually figure out that all she had to do was run to the middle of the stage to get help from the rest of her pirate buddies.

She glanced back at me, and I could see the whites of her eyes. They were afraid and panicked and even looked familiar to me. Too bad she didn't see the stack of wooden boxes directly in front of her.

The moment she hit them, her body flipped into the air like a rag doll, but she miraculously landed on her feet. It wasn't graceful, but it definitely looked like something out of a movie. Reaching for the wall, she steadied herself and took one more look behind her. I noticed a shiny piece of metal drop from her neck.

I started slowing down because I thought she was done for. I was so sure that when she hit those boxes, she'd have to stop running and catch her breath, but I was wrong. She took one look at me as the lights partially lit her face enough that I could recognize her. She turned back and sprinted down the hallway and out of sight.

I wanted to run after her, but I couldn't. My mouth was so dry from my heavy breathing that I had to stop and find water before I died. But even if I had been able to keep running, I don't know if I would have. Because the second I caught a glimpse of the girl's face, I felt like my brain exploded. It was possible that I was a walking zombie, killed by the shock of what I had just seen.

I glanced at the ground, at a small piece of metal that reflected the fluorescent lights above. It was the piece of metal that had dropped from the girl's neck right before she took off again.

I picked it up, inspecting the gold medallion carefully, studying the tiny skull embedded into the surface. It was the mark of a pirate. The other pirates wore them, too. Looking up, I scanned the hallway, exhausted and sad at realizing who it was I had been chasing after . . .

It was Zoe . . . She was a pirate.

PIRATE PENDANT.

MY HAND.

Friday. 7:45 a.m. Homeroom.

I made sure I was the first to homeroom. I wanted to be there to see if Zoe had anything to say for herself, but after the bell rang, she wasn't in the room. It wasn't like her to miss school, even when she's sick, so I knew she had to be avoiding me.

My ex-best friend, Brayden, was there, though. Since there weren't assigned seats, he came early enough to get a seat up front, far away from me. Obviously, he was trying to avoid me as well. I don't blame him.

"Good morning, students," said Mrs. Robinson. "TGIF, right?"

The students murmured.

"You might be too young to understand yet," she said. "Anyway, it's Friday, and the day of Dance Till Ya Drop. You'll be happy to hear that everything planned for it has gone well, and we're bound to have a wonderful night tonight, so I hope that you all tried your best to raise money."

I shifted in my seat, uncomfortable at the thought of Carlyle's plan to change the mascot to a buccaneer.

"Remember that the student with the most money wins the trip to Hawaii and also the chance to change the old and outdated mascot of Buchanan from a wildcat to . . . well, whatever they please. What kind of mascots do you think would be good for Buchanan?"

One of the students shouted an answer. "A bald eagle!"

Another student corrected him. "A bald *dude*!"

"A zombie!"

"A *bald* zombie!"

Mrs. Robinson sighed. "A bald zombie. Y'know, the other teachers said this was a bad idea, and I'm beginning to wonder if they were right."

I nodded my head, agreeing with her.

"Anyway, the event is tonight. Again, if you're not staying after school to help set up the cafeteria, you'll need to have your parents bring you in at four thirty. It'll take some time to sign in. Bring all the money you've collected, which should've been in the form of written checks. We don't want a repeat of the food drive on our hands, do we?"

She was referring to how Wyatt had stolen all the cash from the food drive.

"You'll have to fill out a form or something, and then you'll walk into the cafeteria. The event will start at five o'clock sharp, aaaaaaaand you'll all dance until you drop. At seven o'clock, the money should be counted up, and the winner will be announced at the end of the event!"

Carlyle was sure to win the event. He was going to have all the pirates give him the money that they raised, and he had enough pirates that he would probably dominate as the winner. There was always the chance that an overachiever would upset the contest, but that was doubtful.

Mrs. Robinson continued the morning announcements, but all I heard was "blah blah blah." There was far too much on my mind. My backpack was sitting next to my desk, and inside it were my ninja robes.

I'd decided the night before that I was just going to give up. I know it sounds lame, but there wasn't much else I could do. Carlyle's threat against Zoe walking the plank . . . that was one thing, but after I found out that she had actually *become* a pirate? Well, that was much, *much* worse.

When I first became the ninja leader, I tried to get her to join. Yes, I realize how completely two faced that sounds because I wouldn't let Brayden in automatically. But Zoe was different. She was there when the ninja clan first contacted me and even helped me join. But she told me no when I offered her a place as a ninja.

She was nice about it—she didn't poke fun at me. I think she was genuinely happy to see me become part of a group since I was the new kid at Buchanan. Plus, she had a good excuse—she wanted to participate in other groups like the cheerleading squad or even the volleyball team, which is exactly why it felt like a sucker punch to see her parading around as a pirate.

So that was it. Zoe had chosen her side. Brayden had betrayed me. And I'd lost the entire ninja clan. Some leader I was, huh? In a way, it was sort of a relief. Carlyle would win and the school would become the Buchanan Buccaneers. His vengeance would be complete by that night.

And I wouldn't have the stress of leading a group of sixth-grade ninjas, so I'd be able to sink back into the invisible lifestyle I'd grown accustomed to. It wasn't a big deal. At least I'd have my comic books to keep me company.

Just then the bell rang, signaling the end of homeroom. I'd completely zoned out the entire time. The rest of Mrs. Robinson's announcements had gone right over my head.

I grabbed my bag from the floor and turned to talk to Zoe, but then I remembered she wasn't there. Being late to school was one thing, but for Zoe to miss homeroom completely was actually something to worry about.

Brayden stopped just before exiting the room. "Where's Zoe?"

I shrugged my shoulders. "I dunno. It's not like her to miss any amount of any class."

"Weird," Brayden said before he stepped out of the door.

It *was* weird. A little *too* weird. She'd made her choice to become a pirate, but that didn't make her any less my cousin. I decided that I should try calling her house. My locker is where I kept my cell phone, and yes, this isn't 1990 anymore—kids have cell phones stashed away in the lockers for emergencies . . . what, you don't?

I dialed her home phone number and leaned my head into the inside of my locker so teachers couldn't tell what I was doing. I'm sure I looked suspicious, though. I mean, my entire *head* was in my locker.

Her dad picked up. "Hello?"

"Uncle John? This is Chase. Is Zoe around?"

"Chase? Hey, buddy, what's happening?"

"Oh, not much. Y'know . . . same old, same old, talkin' on a cell phone with my head shoved into a locker."

Uncle John laughed. "Why would you be doing that? You getting picked on again? Aren't you some sort of almighty ninja now? Zoe talks about it all the time."

"She *does?*" I asked, surprised. "I mean, is she around? She wasn't in homeroom today, and that's not really like her, so I got kind of worried."

"That's awfully nice of you, but yeah, I'm afraid she's not feeling too well. She tried going to school this morning, but I told her that if she wanted to make it to the dance tonight, she'd have to stay home and rest first."

"Oh, good," I said. "So she'll be here tonight?"

"Yep."

"Can I talk to her?"

Uncle John paused. "She's actually taking a little nap on the couch, but I can tell her you called when she wakes up. How's that sound?"

"Good," I said. "No need for her to call me back though, since I'm at school. My phone's in my locker so I won't be able to get to it."

"All right. I'll let her know you called," said Uncle John. "She'll appreciate that."

Snapping my phone shut, I tossed it back onto the top shelf of my locker. At least Zoe was all right. If anything, I felt better about that. It also made what I was going to do in gym class all the more easy.

Friday. 10:45 a.m. Gym class.

Not surprising to me, Carlyle wasn't in art class. I'm sure he was probably working on the stage in the cafeteria, building his army of pirates. Brayden was there, though. I gave him a note to hand off to his captain, and he said he would.

Now I'm sitting in the boys' locker room, waiting to see if Brayden actually gave Carlyle the note.

"Chase," said Carlyle's voice.

I guess Brayden did.

I turned around and faced the pirate captain. I wasn't surprised to see Brayden standing next to him. "You weren't in art today, Captain Carlyle."

"I had *better* things to attend to," said Carlyle.

"Skipping class is a good way to get busted."

Carlyle laughed. "Are you warning me or something? Trying to make sure that I don't get in trouble?"

"No," I said. I don't know why I told him that. Maybe I was just nervous, and when I'm nervous, I always talk without thinking.

Carlyle stepped forward with his hands behind his back. "Brayden gave me your note. I assume you've called this meeting here in the locker room because you're ready to admit defeat."

I said nothing.

"It's all right, lad," said Carlyle. "Even the best of us have to fail from time to time. In your case, the time just happens to be at this moment."

I took my book bag off and dropped it on the cement in front of my feet.

Carlyle snapped his fingers, and Brayden stepped forward. He marched over to my book bag and unzipped it. Then he dug his fat hot dog fingers into it and pulled my ninja robes out. Tossing them on the floor in front of the captain, he spoke. "It's all here, Cap'n."

"Good," Carlyle sneered. "Then it's just about finished, isn't it, Chase?"

I couldn't look him in the eye.

Picking up my ninja robes, he turned around and started for the door. "Hope t'see you tonight, matey. It's gonna be a heckuva dance."

I fell to my knees and felt the cold cement through my blue jeans. That was that. It was over for me, but I was numb to it. I think I realized that without Zoe on my team, I just didn't care. Weird, because not caring about something felt the same way as wanting to puke.

Friday night. 4:30 p.m. My dad's car.

My dad had to drop me off at the school that night. I really wasn't keen on going to the dance, but since it was mandatory, I didn't have a choice. I was in the front seat as Dad drove. Of course, I was, what did you think? That I was five years old and still sitting in a baby seat in the back? No way. I'm almost *twelve!*

I pushed my hand into the front pocket of my jeans and felt the skull pendant that Zoe had dropped yesterday. I brought it along so I could confront her with it.

"So you have a date for tonight?" Dad asked.

I shook my head as I stared out the window. "It's not that kind of dance."

"No? I guess I've never heard of any other kind."

"It's to raise money for cardiovascular health or whatever."

"Ah," Dad sighed. "A dance for the ol' ticker."

"And we're supposed to go until we drop."

"Drop dead?"

"Dead tired maybe. I dunno."

"Is there some sort of prize or something?"

"Yeah, but I'm pretty sure some other kid has it in the bag," I said.

"Oh, he's done more work than anyone or something?" Dad asked.

"*Something,*" I repeated. "To be honest, I think that if he wins, it'll be unfair."

"Unfair? How so?"

"Well, I mean, he's only going to win because . . . " I trailed off. Telling my dad about the pirate invasion would've landed me in a loony bin. "Because he cheated."

Dad shook his head. "Not cool. Does anyone else know he cheated?"

"Yeah," I said. "Like, *everyone* does. Everyone except the teachers."

Dad paused. "Want me to say something to them?"

"No!" I said quickly.

Dad nodded. He was good at understanding what I felt when I didn't come out and say it. "So . . . what do you think you're gonna do about it?"

I pulled my foot up and rested it on the dashboard. "I thought maybe something, but what's the point? What's it worth to say anything when everyone knows anyways and actually *wants* him to win?"

The car ride was silent for a moment as Dad pulled into the school's parking lot. I could see several of the other students getting dropped off by the front doors. Many of them were dressed as pirates.

"You didn't mention it was a costume party," Dad said.

"It's not."

When Dad pulled up to the curb to drop me off, he stopped the car and put it in park. Then he turned to me and spoke in a way that almost made him seem like he had experience with this sort of thing. "Chase, listen. I know you're probably confused about this whole thing with that kid winning the prize when he shouldn't. It bums me out a little to hear you say that you probably won't do anything about it. I'm not saying you should sound the alarms or anything, . . . but I hope you do *something*. It's never the popular thing to go against the crowd, but at least you're standing up to it. Think about it—in a world where everyone is following the same path, you're the one who's found the strength to create your own. It might seem scary at first, but trust me, you'll feel free."

Was my dad right? Was it possible that maybe, for once in my entire life, I should actually listen to his advice? Something about what he said gave me comfort. I smiled. "Yeah, good thing I'm already pretty unpopular."

"Look at it this way," Dad said. "It might feel like the world is against you, but it's really *not* that."

"Then what is it?"

"It's that nobody is exactly *with* you," he said. "There's a huge difference there that should give you strength."

Sometimes my dad made too much sense. "Whatever," I said with a half smile. He knew I understood.

Dad laughed and rubbed my head in a way he knew I hated. "Now get outta my car. Text me when it's almost over and I'll come back out . . . *maybe*."

I mocked a laugh at him as I stepped onto the curb with my yellow envelope of fundraiser money. "Har, har."

As he pulled away, I turned to face Buchanan School. The whole front entrance was packed with kids talking and joking around. I couldn't see Zoe anywhere yet, but her dad had said that she'd be here.

Shouts of pirate insults drifted through the air toward me Seriously, I *hate* when people talk like pirates.

Friday. 4:40 p.m. Buchanan School lobby.

I waited my turn in line among a sea of costumed children. To be honest, I can understand why some kids would get so into it. They get to come to school dressed in baggy clothing that look like pajamas *and* they don't have to worry about their grammar—it *does* sound appealing. But was it necessary for many of them to stop bathing altogether? The lobby of the school stank like moldy cheese.

"Yar, mate," said a boy in front of me. "Top of the mornin' to ya!"

"You sound like a leprechaun," I said. "Not a pirate."

"That be the best part, no?" he asked, at least I *think* it was a question. "We pirates live by one rule, and that's to live by *no* rules!"

My brain really felt like it was worn out from having to translate all the gibberish coming from this kid's mouth, so I had to just smile and nod at him slowly.

"Chase, your envelope, please," said the teacher manning the sign-in table. It was Mr. Cooper.

I handed him my yellow envelope. As I filled out the slip of paper with my name and stuff, Mr. Cooper opened the envelope and dumped the contentsonto the table.

"You only got one check?" he asked.

"Mm-hmm," I hummed.

"And it's from your parents," he added.

"That's right," I said.

Mr. Cooper sighed. "Well, at least it's more than the other kids so far."

"What do you mean?"

The coach leaned across the table and spoke under his voice. "Nobody else raised a single penny. They've all handed in *empty* envelopes. It's rather disappointing to say the least."

I didn't speak. Mr. Cooper thought nobody raised any money, but I knew the truth. Everyone had already given Carlyle their earnings so he could win the prize. Biting my lip, I said, "Weird."

"It is," Mr. Cooper said as he took the sheet of paper with my name on it. Then he pointed at the cafeteria doors. "Welcome to the party."

The inside of the cafeteria was dark. The staff had blocked the windows with large dividers so that the disco lights near the ceiling could do their job. A blaze of blue and pink colors danced on the walls as loud bass music shook the ground. When I opened the door, it was like walking into a wall of hot air. A wall of hot air that *stank*.

Mrs. Robinson was standing just inside the door. She was holding a napkin in one hand and a half-eaten cookie in the other while she moved her body slightly to the deafeningly loud music.

When she saw me, she laughed as if I'd caught her doing something she wasn't supposed to be doing. "Hi, Chase!" she said loudly. "Cookies and punch are on the table in the back of the room."

"Thanks!" I replied. I had no intention of actually dancing, so I was happy to hear there was a table I could hang around.

As I made my way across the cafeteria, I could see that almost everyone was here already. A lot of the kids must have stayed after school to help set up the room. The most discouraging part about it was that *every single kid* was dressed as a pirate except for me. If that didn't make me stick out like a sore thumb, I don't know what else would.

I recognized a couple of the pirates. They used to be part of my ninja clan. When I made eye contact though, they looked away. Maybe *they* were embarrassed, but I couldn't help but feel like they were disappointed in me.

Zoe was supposed to be at the dance, but I still hadn't seen her at this point. I had no idea what I would say to her if I saw her, but I knew it wasn't going to be nice things.

Finally, I reached the table of cookies and punch. Kids in dumb-looking pirate costumes huddled around it, munching on fat chocolate chip cookies and spilling red juice all over the floor. There was no way I was going to push through the crowd of pirate kids, so I took a spot on the wall, leaning against it. I did this for about forty-five minutes, watching carefully for any signs of Zoe.

Friday. 5:30 p.m. Dance Till Ya Drop.

At this point in the dance, it just felt like I was at someone's Halloween party, except I was the only one who didn't get the memo that it had a pirate theme.

Carlyle had arrived and was out in the middle of the dance floor. Say what you want about the kid, but he was definitely a charmer. Girls were lined up for a turn to dance with their captain.

"Pretty gross, isn't it?" said a voice from right next to me.

I turned to face the kid. I was surprised to see it was Zoe, dressed in a silly-looking pirate costume. "You've got a lot of nerve," I said.

Zoe looked confused. "Huh? What're you *talking* about?"

I shook my head. "Look at what you're wearing! You've chosen which side you want to be on! Just like Brayden and everyone else in this school! You're such a sheep."

"A sheep?" she said, upset. "How am I a sheep?"

"You're following the crowd without using your brain!" I explained. "You're not even *thinking* straight right now. I *know* it was you I was chasing yesterday."

"Chase, you'd better hang onto that tongue of yours," she sneered. "I think it's running pretty wild right now."

"We're *family!* Family is supposed to stick together, but you abandoned me!" I started laughing in a way that made me feel like a villain. "I offered you a spot in my ninja clan, and you refused because you were too cool for it! No thanks, you said! I'd like to spend my time playing volleyball and cheering for the football team, you said! But look at you now! Dressed like a frumpy pirate lost in the crowd!"

Zoe didn't say anything, but I could see that she was really angry. So angry that it looked like tears were forming in her eyes. Wait . . . do tears form when people get mad?

I started talking again, but she turned and walked away before I could get the words out. "I'm sor—"

"Nice," said one of the pirates who overheard our conversation. When I looked, I saw that the entire crowd of pirates around me had heard the whole thing.

Carlyle stepped forward. "Seems as though you do quite good at destroying *yourself.*"

I didn't speak. The music thumped and trembled the floor of the cafeteria as pirates circled around me. I've read a lot about situations like this in ninja training. When surrounded by a group of attackers, . . . it's best to get yourself out of there. Pretty obvious, right?

"Tonight, you'll bear witness to my victory," Carlyle said as he gestured for his minions to close in and tighten their circle. He knew I was trying to get out of it.

"These kids have a right to know your intentions," I said.

The captain laughed loudly. "They already *do!* That's the most beautiful part! They *want* to help me win!"

"You want to be led by a maniac?" I asked the crowd. "You want this kid to win the prize *just* because he's a smooth talker?"

Many of the students nodded. I could see they wouldn't be convinced easily.

"What's your endgame here, mate?" Carlyle asked. "What d'you think you'll accomplish right now? The entire school be against ya!"

"It's not that anyone is *against* me," I said.

Was I really about to quote my dad?

"It's just that nobody is exactly *with* me."

Yep. I just quoted my dad.

The music playing in the background suddenly scratched to a stop, and then a girl's voice shouted from somewhere in the cafeteria. "*I'm* with you!"

At that moment, the curtain to the stage started peeling open, revealing all the work that the pirates had done that week. The Buchanan Buccaneers flag was pinned to the back wall. In front of that was a medium sized, crudely created boat that was probably supposed to be a pirate ship. At the side of the stage stood Zoe, hanging onto the rope that drew open the curtain. Many of the pirates gasped, in awe of the ship.

I didn't know what to say.

"What's the point of exposing this?" Carlyle asked. "These kids already know what the plan is!"

Zoe ran to the front of the stage and spoke to the crowd of listening students. "Do you really know what this will do to Buchanan if he changes our mascot from the Wildcats to the Buccaneers?"

There were some murmurs throughout the crowd.

"I think they do," Carlyle shouted. "Doesn't seem like they mind much, either."

"You're just giving power to a different kind of bully!" Zoe said. "His intentions aren't just to win this thing."

This was when Carlyle started to grow angry. He started walking toward the stage. "You'll hold your tongue if ya know what's good for ya, lassie!"

Zoe folded her arms. "I'll do no such thing. This boy is Wyatt's cousin! Changing the mascot to the Buccaneers is his own weird way of taking over Buchanan! It's his plan to rule over it as the pirate captain! Is this really the kid you want choosing our new mascot?"

"I said hold your tongue, or you're gonna be very sorry!" Carlyle shouted, now running full speed toward the stage.

But many of the students didn't move for him. They stood their ground, blocking him from my cousin.

"Is what she's sayin' true?" asked one of the girl pirates. "Are you really Wyatt's cousin? Is this all just some kind of revenge game for you?"

"I needn't answer to a scallywag like you!" Carlyle said. "It doesn't matter anyhow, I'm already the winner of the contest, and in a little bit, you'll see that my plan has become complete!"

I ran to the stage. "Zoe," I said. "But you . . . I thought . . . "

Zoe tightened the side of her mouth and shook her head at me. "You numbskull . . . don't you remember what I said last Monday?"

I thought as hard as I could but couldn't recall. I shook my head.

"I said I've always got your back . . . no matter what. Even if it means going deep undercover."

I glanced at her pirate uniform. Then I pulled the skull pendant from my pocket. "You were undercover as a pirate?"

A smile beamed across her face as she nodded her head at me. She really *was* the coolest cousin in the world. "Yesterday, I ran from you because if any of these pirates saw us talking, my cover would've been blown. I joined the pirates to see for myself what they were doing."

"So this morning," I said. "You weren't skipping school to avoid me?"

Zoe nodded. "Oh yeah, I totally skipped to avoid you. I'm terrible at lying and I knew if you confronted me about it, I would've caved."

"I feel like an idiot," I said to her.

"Ya look like one too, matey!" Carlyle shouted. "None of this changes the fact that you're all finished! The school is mine, and Wyatt's revenge is complete! When he returns to this school, it'll be ours for the taking!"

"When he *returns* to this school?" I asked. Why would Carlyle say such a thing? Wyatt was expelled, which meant no do-overs.

The lights in the cafeteria flickered on as some of the teachers stepped onto the dance floor. Mr. Cooper was leading the pack of adults. He wore a stupid-looking grin on his face.

"Students," he shouted. "I'm sorry to interrupt . . . " he trailed off, confused by all the pirates standing by a stage that had a pirate ship on it. Shaking his head, he continued. "Um, weird. Anyways,

I'm sorry to interrupt whatever *this* is, but it seems we have a clear winner for the event tonight."

"Keep your earballs peeled, boy," Carlyle sneered at me.

Mr. Cooper extended his arm and pointed straight at the pirate captain. "*Carlyle* has won the prize. He raised the most money out of all the entries tonight!"

Zoe jumped down from the stage. "How much did he win by? What were the totals?"

Mr. Cooper laughed. "Normally we wouldn't give out that information, but in this case, I think it's all right. There were only two students who actually raised any money at all." The coach pointed at me. "Chase collected exactly five dollars."

"And how much did Carlyle raise?" Zoe asked.

"Eleven thousand, two hundred twenty-two dollars, and fifty cents," Mr. Cooper said.

"Seriously?" Zoe shouted. "That doesn't seem a little strange to you?"

Mr. Cooper put his hand on his hip and crinkled his brow, thinking for a moment. Finally, he answered. "No. Not at all."

Carlyle punched me in the chest. Probably a victory punch. It wasn't hard, but it hurt. "Game over! You lost, Chase! You've lost *everything!* Your friends! Your ninja clan! Your school! Just wait until Wyatt hears about this!"

My head started spinning again. The room became a blur of bright colors and faces as Carlyle continued to celebrate his victory by jumping up and down and laughing. Zoe was off to the side, walking toward me.

"You can't let it end like this! You can't!" she said.

"What can I do?" I asked, trying to keep from falling over. My knees felt weak.

"Anything! You can't let this psychopath change the mascot! Do something! Anything!"

Some of the students behind me put their hands on my shoulder. I heard some familiar voices from my ninja clan.

"Master," a boy said. "You mustn't give in!"

Another voice spoke. "Please, we've made a terrible mistake. We let our boredom get to us! Our need for excitement blinded us!"

"But I failed you as a leader," I whispered.

One of the girls stood in front of me and looked me in the eye. "No," she said. "You were a better leader than we knew. Look at you. You're the *only one* in this gym that's not dressed as a pirate!"

"I'm *undercover*," Zoe snipped.

The same boy that talked to me after my fight with Wyatt spoke. "It's the same as before. You stood your ground and made the choice to do good. And for that alone, you deserve to be the leader."

"I don't have my ninja robe anymore," I said.

The boy tapped at my chest. "But you're a ninja in here. Besides, those robes are cheap. We have tons of extras that haven't even been opened yet. Just take one of those during the next meeting."

Suddenly, Zoe slapped my face.

"Hey!" I said as I clutched my cheek.

"You're a ninja again! Now quit feeling sorry for yourself and get our school back!" shouted my cousin.

The members of my ninja clan punched their open palms and bowed to me. The room suddenly stopped spinning, and my heart started racing. I jumped to my feet and stared at Carlyle. He was still doing his victory dance. "Hey!"

Carlyle turned to face me. "What is it, loser?"

"You won this event by cheating!" I said. "And I demand a rematch!"

"What?" Carlyle asked. "Is someone a sore loser?"

"No," I said. "I'm not. I just know that you'd lose in a match against me."

"What kind of match?" Carlyle asked, interested. "I've already won. Tell me why I'd want to keep playing with a mouse like you?"

"Because you can't *stop* yourself," I said, narrowing my eyes. "Victory tastes too sweet for you to *not* risk everything you've already achieved."

Carlyle stepped forward, silent for a second. "What be the stakes, matey?"

"You can have your trip to Hawaii," I said. "But if I win, then you give *me* the power to change the school's mascot."

The captain tapped at his chin. "And if you lose?"

"I'll switch schools," I said.

Zoe and my ninja clan gasped.

"Tell me that wouldn't be the greatest revenge," I said, looking directly into the eyes of the captain. "You take my friends, my ninja clan, and my school . . . *plus* I never return to Buchanan."

Carlyle laughed. He looked at Mr. Cooper the way a dog does when they want to go outside.

The coach lifted his hand and waved. "I'll allow it."

"Good," I said. "Meet me at the Norwegian obstacle course in five minutes."

Friday. Five minutes later. Norwegian obstacle course.

The entire school followed us down to the track where the obstacle course was set up. Most of the students had removed their pirate costumes, but a few stragglers remained confident that Carlyle would win.

"Are you sure you know what you're doing?" Zoe asked.

I shook my head as I approached the starting line. "Nope."

"You fell off the second obstacle last time," said a voice.

I turned around and was met by Brayden. He wasn't wearing his pirate hat anymore. "Man, I'm sorry about what I did to you."

I didn't speak.

"I let it all go to my head," he said. "You didn't let me join your ninja clan, and Carlyle said I could be a pirate if I wanted to. I just . . . I guess I chose poorly."

"I *should've* let you in," I said. "It was dumb of me not to. I just wasn't sure of what kind of leader I could be, and I made some poor decisions."

"You seem to be doing just fine as a leader right now," he said, smirking.

"We'll see," I said. "If I lose, then everything is still under Carlyle's control."

"At this point, I think everyone has seen that you've stood against him," Brayden said. "That's a sure sign that your leadership skills can pay some bills, y'know?"

I raised my fist to Brayden, and he bumped it with his own. That was the guy way of saying things were cool.

"Wait," I said as I looked at Zoe. "If Zoe was *already* a pirate, then what was all the talk about making her walk the plank?"

"*You were gonna make me walk to the plank?*" Zoe asked, angry.

Brayden put his hands up in surrender and shook his head. "No! No no no, that was all just a bluff. We knew you had no idea she was a pirate, so the bluff sorta worked."

"*Double agent pirate,*" Zoe corrected.

"Quit your talking!" Carlyle shouted as he approached the starting line.

Mr. Cooper joined us. "This Norwegian monster is impossible to beat, so that's not what you'll be racing for. First one that gets knocked out by it is the loser. You probably should've filled out the paperwork saying you won't sue the school, but . . . oh well."

That helped me feel a little better. I didn't need to make it to the end. I just had to last longer than Carlyle did.

A gun popped from above as Mr. Cooper raised his arm. Apparently, it was the sign to go because Carlyle had already started climbing up to the rope bridge.

"Go!" Zoe cried.

I grabbed the ropes and started climbing after Carlyle. He was already several feet above me. He had even started crossing the rope path that led to the rock wall about ten feet away. I gripped tighter and started moving faster.

"You're already losing!" Carlyle shouted.

I wanted to yell back, but was too focused on not falling. As soon as I pulled myself up onto the rope path, I began carefully stepping each foot over the other.

The pirate captain was already standing at the spot where I fell the first time I tried playing on this thing. It was a short hop to the rock wall from where he was standing.

He stopped long enough for me to catch up to him. "That wall looks far," I said.

"Ladies first," Carlyle replied.

I took a breath and judged the distance between the wall and the bridge. It wasn't far, but the first time I jumped last Monday, I missed the handholds. Closing my eyes, I nodded, and then jumped into the unknown.

"He jumped with his eyes closed!" shouted one of the kids from the crowd.

Suddenly I heard the entire school burst with applause as I sailed through the air. It was as if time slowed down. I heard the other students cheering me on, shouting and hollering at me. My eyes shot open, and I saw Zoe covering her face, unable to watch my jump. Brayden was frozen in time with his jaw dropped and eyes peeled wide open. I even felt like I had enough time to glance back at Carlyle. The pirate captain was angrier than I'd ever seen as he watched me reach for the handholds.

I turned back around and reached my fingers out. They grazed the handholds of the rock wall and slipped off. No, I thought. Not again! As I started slipping down, I kicked my feet out and just happened to catch one of the handholds below me. It was just enough to give me another shot at grabbing the wall with my hands.

And it worked.

I gripped tightly and pulled my body against the wall. Everybody cheered again. Everyone except for Carlyle. He was behind me hurling insults in my direction.

"Oh, no you don't!" Carlyle shouted as he jumped from the rope path, flailing his arms wildly toward the wall.

I could already tell this was going to end badly.

The captain's hands landed on the wall but couldn't find anything to grip. His body was still moving at full steam as he smashed against the surface. For a second, time stopped again, and I could see his fear when we made eye contact. Then he plummeted to the pool of water below. I heard the splash as his body hit the water.

The crowd of spectators shouted at the tops of their lungs, rejoicing in my victory over the captain. A part of me felt sorry for him, but that didn't last long.

"You rotten ninja!" Carlyle cried out, splashing in the water. "You think this is the last you've heard of me?"

I climbed down from the wall and looked at him. "The mascot is mine to change," I said coldly. "You've lost."

"I take it back!" Carlyle laughed. "This was all just a joke! Buchanan will still be called the Buccaneers!"

"I'm afraid not," said Mr. Cooper. "A deal's a deal, and you said Chase can have the opportunity to change our mascot."

"Fool!" Carlyle shouted. "You think you've won, do you? *You think this is over?*"

I looked at the defeated pirate. "I *know* it's not."

For now, the mascot was safe, and that was enough for me to let myself feel happy. A few old members of my ninja clan approached me.

"With respect," said one of the boys. "We'd like to rejoin if you'd allow us."

I shrugged my shoulders. "I don't know how different it's going to be from the last time you guys were in it."

"We wouldn't have you change a thing," said one of the girls next to him. "You've proven *twice* that you're worthy of the calling. You stood up to Wyatt, *and* you saved our school from a pirate invasion."

"I think it's important to point out that he stood up to Carlyle too," said Brayden.

The girl nodded. "Yes. That too."

"We await your answer," the boy said.

"Of course, I'll still be your leader!" I said. "Why wouldn't I be?"

Punching their palms, they bowed. And then they turned and walked away. It was weird how they did that so often.

"So are we going to be called the Buchanan Ninjas?" Zoe asked.

I shook my head. "Nah, I'm not sure what it's going to be, but I don't think our mascot should be a ninja."

"Unicorns?" Zoe suggested.

I laughed so loud that I snorted. Brayden and Zoe made fun of me, playfully punching at my arm as they did. The rest of the students had started walking back to the school, and Mr. Cooper was probably back in his office by then.

I turned back to see what Carlyle was doing, but when I looked, he was gone. Disappeared without a trace. Well, I'm sure there was some type of trace, but I didn't care enough to search.

"Go on, guys," I said. "I'll catch up."

I let Zoe and Brayden walk ahead of me as I glanced back at the sun setting in the sky. It had been a crazy week, but at the end of it, I wouldn't have it any other way. I was still the leader of the ninja clan, which I was grateful for, but at that moment, I swore to work harder at the job. If there was any truth to what Carlyle had said—that Wyatt was returning to this school—I knew we had to be ready.

I've only been at Buchanan for a month, but I've already defeated two bullies and prevented an all-out pirate invasion. There are still eight months of sixth grade left . . .

I wonder what other adventures I'll have while I'm here.

Stories—what an incredible way to open one's mind to a fantastic world of adventure. It's my hope that this story has inspired you in some way, lighting a fire that maybe you didn't know you had. Keep that flame burning no matter what. It represents your sense of adventure and creativity, and that's something nobody can take from you. Thanks for reading! If you enjoyed this book, I ask that you help spread the word by sharing it or leaving an honest review!

– Marcus

m@MarcusEmerson.com

MARCUS EMERSON is the author and illustrator of a whole lot of books including the way popular DIARY OF A 6TH GRADE NINJA series, THE SUPER LIFE OF BEN BRAVER series, and the KID YOUTUBER series. His goal is to create children's books that are funny and inspirational for kids of all ages—even the adults who never grew up.

Marcus still dreams of becoming an astronaut and WALKING ON THE SUN, LIKE WHAT?? THAT'S NOT EVEN POSSIBLE.